ASK CLICK AND CLACK

ASK CLICK AND CLACK
Answers from Car Talk

CAMBRIDGE POLICE LINEUP

DISTURBING THE PEACE

TELLING BAD JOKES

Tom and Ray Magliozzi
Click and Clack, the Tappet Brothers

CHRONICLE BOOKS
SAN FRANCISCO

Library of Congress Cataloging-in-Publication Data:

Magliozzi, Tom.
   Ask Click and Clack : answers from Car talk / by Tom and Ray Magliozzi.
      p. cm.
   Includes index.
   "Click and Clack, the Tappet Brothers."
   ISBN 978-0-8118-6477-0
   1. Automobiles—Anecdotes. 2. Automobiles—Maintenance and repair—Miscellanea. 3. American wit and humor. I. Magliozzi, Ray. II. Car talk (Radio program) III. Title.

   TL146.5.M325 2008
   629.28'72—dc22

                              2008010674

Manufactured in the United States of America

Design by Henry Quiroga
Typeset in FS Albert, HTF Acropolis, & Ketchupa

Thanks to Trish Anderton, in Car Talk's Jakarta office.

See Chronicle Books' full range of Car Talk book and gift titles at www.chroniclebooks.com/cartalk. Additional copies of this book, along with CDs, shirts, and other official Car Talk junk, are available online via the Shameless Commerce Division of the Car Talk Web site at www.cartalk.com.

Chronicle Books LLC
680 Second Street
San Francisco, CA 94107
www.chroniclebooks.com

CONTENTS

Introduction — 6

Chapter 1: THE PERFECT CAR FOR A PIZZA GUY: MOMENTOUS PURCHASING DECISIONS — 11

Chapter 2: HOW CAN I RUIN DAD'S MINIVAN? THE PERILOUS INTERSECTION OF KIDS, PARENTS, AND CARS — 23

Chapter 3: IT'S NOT A PUPPY: CARE AND FEEDING OF YOUR CAR — 41

Chapter 4: MOTOR HONEY FOR YOUR CHARIOT: MYTHS, GIMMICKS, QUACKS, AND OTHER AUTOMOTIVE SKULDUGGERY — 59

Chapter 5: THE FIRST SPARK PLUG ON THE MOON: CURIOUS CAR CONUNDRUMS — 75

Chapter 6: SACRED MALE BONDING RITUALS: THE TRUTH ABOUT GUYS AND CARS — 97

Chapter 7: THE KARMANN GHIA OF HEARTBREAK: CARS AND RELATIONSHIPS — 111

Chapter 8: YOU MAY NEVER HAVE A CHANCE TO DO ANYTHING THIS STUPID AGAIN! IN DEFENSE OF IMPRACTICALITY AND FOLLOWING YOUR HEART — 131

Chapter 9: THE RAT WORE PLAID: HORROR STORIES FROM THE SHOWROOM FLOOR — 145

Chapter 10: TWO TRUCKS ARE CHEAPER THAN ONE: AND OTHER WACKO THEORIES — 155

Chapter 11: WHAT'S THE PLURAL OF "LEXUS"? THE REALLY BIG QUESTIONS — 175

Chapter 12: QUESTIONABLE CAR-MA: ISSUES OF AUTOMOTIVE ETIQUETTE — 191

Car Talk Staff — 202

Index — 206

INTRODUCTION

by Doug Berman, "Esteemed" Producer

You're probably familiar with the *Car Talk* radio show on NPR. Well, back in 1989, Tom and Ray also launched a biweekly newspaper column, called "Click and Clack." The column is a lot like the radio show, except that while providing answers on the radio requires quick reflexes and instantaneous recall, the newspaper columns call for research and deep thought. Whereas the radio show can address a dozen questions in an hour, it often takes up to an hour per question for the column.

Typically, we get together at the studios of WBUR in Boston. We used to have our own office there, but that's since been squatted and eventually acquired by a female news executive who keeps it so clean we don't even recognize it anymore. So we'll sit in the lunchroom or an empty meeting room, or, in emergencies, one each in the three adjoining stalls in the men's room.

This is what's known as "The Monday Meeting." It takes place every Tuesday. We used to meet on Mondays, but even after we moved the meeting to Tuesdays, the original name stuck. The reason we decided to keep the "Monday Meeting" name is that when there's a Monday holiday, we can cancel the Monday meeting, even though the meeting is on Tuesday.

The first order of business in the meeting is waiting for Tom and Ray to show up. One of the guys is always late: traffic, can't find a parking space, car wouldn't start. We start an average of 15 minutes late. Then there's the gathering of coffee. Because there are inevitably people to talk to in the lunchroom, with Tom and Ray, the process of adding cream and sugar can take another 15 minutes.

Next on the agenda: the sharing of symptoms. Colds, runny noses, backaches, lack of sleep, too much sleep, excessive flatulence . . . it all gets covered. Once everyone has complained sufficiently and been dismissed as a whiner by the others, we can move on to the work at hand—answering questions from readers.

We start by looking at the answers we wrote the previous week. I will have taken notes, pounded the various pieces of information into a coherent answer, and will be bringing it back for a final review.

"We said *this*?" asks Tom. "We didn't say this. You made this up."

"I didn't make it up. That's what you said."

"We wouldn't say this. You've got your head up your keister."

Clearly, there was some miscommunication the previous week.

"We might have said this," adds Ray. "But it's wrong."

We rework the column produced last week until the guys are satisfied that hate mail will be minimized, and we move on to this week's work.

Questions pour in by the thousands. The submissions are narrowed down first by lackeys on our staff, and then by me, as I pick a handful of questions I think may be interesting to the guys and to our audience. I'll read the question out loud and record the ensuing discussion on my iPod for later reference.

I read the day's first question. Tom starts to offer his thoughts, and Ray can't remember whether the car in question has disc brakes or drum brakes in the back. So he grabs the phone to call over to the garage. Another five minutes go by as Ray tries to re–figure out how to get an outside line.

Ray reaches his garage manager, Craig, insults his girth and parentage in one phrase, and inquires as to his general well-being and the state of chaos at the shop. Ten minutes later, after they've covered the various advantages of South Beach over Key West, we have an answer: It depends. Depends on the trim level. So we have to answer both ways.

As we finally get rolling on an answer, our pal Luan pokes his head in. He has some bagels he stole for us from the general manager's Donor's Circle reception. "Come on in, Luan!" Luan is Albanian, but that's close enough to Italian that a discussion of carpentry and pastries must take place. Fifteen minutes go by before we get back to work. Keep in mind that we have to write at least two columns a week.

I read the second question I've selected for this week. Bill Littlefield, host of *Only a Game*, pops in and waits to be invited to help himself to a bagel. Now he's eating, and it would be rude to throw him out with his mouth full, so a discussion ensues about which one of us is the worst dressed. No consensus is reached. The truth is, Tom and Ray are colorblind, and they often go around critiquing wardrobes while dressed in orange-and-green plaid. Littlefield puts up with it for the bagel. He leaves.

Ready to do the second column? Wait. Bathroom break. More chat in the hallway. A BUR reporter has another question about her Subaru. Our associate producer, David, pops in to tell us we need to record a promo for WWUW, which will require 16 takes because of the unfortunate call letters. We finally address the second question. Fortunately it's an easy one, because Ray is parked at a two-hour meter and needs to skedaddle. He also wants to swap test cars with somebody. Undoubtedly because he's out of gas. No one bites.

What you're about to read is the result of this rigorous process. At least now you understand why this book costs as much as it does. Look at all the hours we put into it!

THE PERFECT CAR FOR A

PIZZA

GUY

Momentous
Purchasing Decisions

THE PERFECT CAR FOR A PIZZA GUY

Dear Tom and Ray:

I recently left a career as a pizza-delivery driver to work for an architectural photographer. It involved changing cities and giving up what little social life I had. In short, I'm rethinking the decision, and thinking about going back to the pizza business. My question for you folks is this: The vehicle I bought for my new job is much too nice to use for delivering pizzas. It's an almost new VW GTI VR6 (vroom vroom). Plus, I won't be able to afford the payments on my pizza salary. So, if I'm going to return to the night shift at my old job, I'm going to need a cheap car that gets reasonable gas mileage (low 20s to high teens is OK) and is relatively easy to work on. I can spend about $7,000, and I'm pretty handy with a wrench. I was thinking about a Toyota, because I hear they are very reliable. Any help you can offer would be appreciated, and if you're ever in Gainesville, Florida, and get hungry, give Five Star a call and tell them Bo sent you.

—Bo

Tom: What happened, Bo? Not as many women answering the door in their nightgowns in the architectural-photography business?

Ray: You definitely need something much more pathetic-looking if you want any chance of getting decent tips. If the pizza-delivery guy is driving a nicer car than the guy who's buying the pizza, you're going to have a tough time getting sympathy.

Tom: You certainly could buy a Toyota Corolla. They're easy to find, reliable, and economical. And you can probably get a five- or six-year-old one for $7,000. You really can't go wrong with one of those, and it meets all your requirements.

Ray: But why not really go for the sympathy, Bo? I see you in a 1987 Hyundai Excel, blue smoke belching out the back from bad rings . . . one headlight working.

Tom: Plus, it's got vinyl seats, so you can just wipe up the melted mozzarella and spilled tomato sauce. Try doing that with your beautiful Toyota velour!

THE SLEEK BLACK (FORMER) BEAUTY

Dear Tom and Ray:

If you could have any car, new or old, what would it be?

—Rich

Tom: It would be a black 1965 AMC Ambassador convertible, to replace the one my brother crushed one day when I wasn't looking. I called that car my "sleek black beauty," and I had asked my brother to watch it for a few days at the garage, and when I came back to get it, he had sent it to the crusher! I'll never forgive him for it.

Ray: It wasn't a few days, it was eight months. And the reason he left it at the garage is because it didn't run anymore. It was a complete heap. There were dogs living in it. It was scaring away customers. It was an act of mercy to send it to the crusher. And he didn't even NOTICE that it was gone for over a month.

Tom: I categorically deny your allegations . . . except the one about the dogs. There was a nice shepherd family living in there. But you owe me a '65 Ambassador convertible.

Ray: Well then, I guess if I could have any car, it would also have to be a black '65 AMC Ambassador convertible . . . so I could give it to my brother and shut him up about this once and for all.

TOM AND RAY'S OWN CARS

Dear Tom and Ray:

After listening to your radio show and reading your column for years, I have come to the conclusion that you must be two of the greatest auto experts alive. Since you can solve other people's problems without even looking at their cars, your own cars must always be in tip-top condition. I am also sure that they never break down, because you fix the problems as soon as they occur—perhaps sometimes even before they happen. Would you, therefore, mind telling me which cars you drive yourself? Because I am absolutely positive that they must be the most well engineered, reliable, comfortable, fuel-efficient, and cost-effective cars one can buy, and I would like to get one myself.

—Dave

Ray: Do I detect a hint of sarcasm, Dave?

Tom: Oh, no!

Ray: Well, since you asked, Dave, I currently drive a 1997 Honda Odyssey, which was one of the "small" Odysseys, before Honda turned it into a full-blown minivan.

Tom: I used to drive a 1952 MG TD, which met every one of your criteria, except for well engineered, reliable, comfortable, fuel-efficient, and cost-effective. But I parked it at my brother-in-law's last year, and now I take the bus or Green Line train everywhere. And both of those do meet every one of your criteria, Dave. And, of particular importance to me, I never have to work on either of them on weekends!

YOU THINK YOU HAVE A BAD CAR!

Dear Tom and Ray:

When you want to use a throwaway example of a really bad car, you always say "my brother's '63 Dodge Dart." In your serious opinion (if you have such), is that really the worst car ever? How about those little Chevys with the motor in the rear? Those AMC Pacers that were as wide as they were long? Those little Fords that exploded if hit in the rear by a shopping cart? I'd be interested in your considered opinion.

—Dee

Tom: Great question, Dee. I think we'll need to split our awards into categories, because there are many different dimensions of "bad." You've got aesthetics, performance, comfort, and reliability, just to name a few.

Ray: Let's start with aesthetics. When you talk about the ugliest cars ever made, you can't avoid the three initials AMC. American Motors made the Pacer, the Hornet, the Gremlin, the Concord, and the list goes on . . . and on. Each of these designs had to pass a homeliness test before they let it out the door. In fact, I'm convinced that AMC had industrial espionage agents going through the wastebaskets at Ford and GM to steal the designs they threw away. Then AMC would sit on them for ten years and let them ferment.

Tom: My vote for the worst-performing car of all time would have to go to the VW Diesel Rabbit. Talk about a dog! There were generally two presidential elections held in the time it took this car to go from 0 to 60.

Ray: VW also takes home a trophy in the discomfort category. In particular, the nod goes to the old air-cooled Volkswagen Microbus. Not only have I ridden camels that made my butt less sore, but you could never get enough heat in the winter. And because the passenger compartment was so big, your body heat would never make a difference. In the Microbus, you'd need a family of panting Saint Bernards with you to keep the temperature above freezing.

Tom: And finally, we get to our most competitive category, reliability. Our winner has to be Fiat. You've heard of the high-school equivalency diploma, right? Well, owning a Fiat gave you a mechanical equivalency degree. When you went to apply for a mechanic's job, they asked, "Where have you worked before?" And if you said, "I owned a Fiat," they said, "Great. When can you start?"

Ray: And as for the '63 Dodge Dart, to set the record straight, it was not a terrible car for its time. It's my brother's car in particular that is an unmitigated piece of junk.

A LITTLE PICK-ME-UP

Dear Tom and Ray:

I am considering buying a pickup truck. I know the advantages, but would you please outline the disadvantages of buying a truck with a diesel engine?

—Ole

Ray: You know the advantages of buying a pickup truck? Please let me know! I've been trying to explain to my wife why I bought one for almost six years now.

Tom: Of course there are advantages, Ole. A pickup truck seats only two people. So whenever our families go out, my brother can always say, "Gee, Tom, I guess we'll have to take your car again." That saves a lot of wear and tear.

Ray: The disadvantage is that sometimes you have to carry more than one passenger, especially if you have kids. And I know my wife is getting awfully tired of riding in the cargo bed . . . especially in the winter.

Tom: Another advantage is that—as the name implies—you can "pick up" stuff.

Ray: But as I discovered after I bought my pickup, every place delivers! And worse, people you hardly even know—people who are friends of friends of friends—will ask to borrow your truck whenever they need to move anything. And they'll ask you to help.

Tom: As far as engines go, diesels are great if you have that backwoods survivalist mentality. A diesel engine is a perfect complement to the bomb shelter in your backyard and the 5,872 cans of chicken noodle soup in your pantry. Diesel fuel can be stored indefinitely, so you'll always be prepared. And diesel engines don't need spark plugs, so when nuclear winter wipes out all electronics, you'll be able to push-start your pickup and head right out to Sears for their 50 percent off "after-nuclear-winter" sale.

Ray: But on the other hand, the older generation of diesels is noisy, smelly, dirty, sluggish, and hard to start in cold weather. So I'd opt for a gasoline engine. I know we'll hear from the diesel fanatics out there, but gasoline is definitely the way to go.

• **Editor's note:** Since this column was written in 1993, diesels have become a more viable, cleaner option—although pickups have not.

THE WIND IN YOUR BALD SPOT

Dear Tom and Ray:

I've always wanted an Aston Martin—no kidding. And now, at age seventy-two, my wife (who is younger) says it's OK for me to buy or lease one. But . . . I feel oh so guilty. To spend that kind of money on a toy—albeit a sumptuous one—seems, well, immoral (and the Vantage gets a measly 13 mpg city). I currently drive an Acura TL, a very quick, very nice car. The lease is up soon. HELP! Should I accept my wife's offer—or is she just testing me? ("How irresponsible of you. What am I going to do with that thing later?" In this context, "later" has a very dark meaning.)

—Michael

P.S. I love your column and radio show. I used to write books with athletes, so I got to scrimmage with the New York Giants and the Los Angeles Lakers, and to hit against Bob Gibson. Also, in an abortive relationship for a book about racing, I got to register the slowest elapsed time ever recorded at Indy. A "blistering" 55.365 mph. How slow is that? So slow that the car started to slide down the side of the banked north turn.

Tom: Michael, go for it. Get your Aston Martin.

Ray: I agree. You sound like a reasonable guy, and you're not going to be a danger to anyone on the road.

Tom: You've always wanted one. What are you waiting for?

Ray: If your conscience really is bothered by the gasoline consumption, just drive less. If you drive ten miles in your Acura, you'll probably use the same amount of fuel that driving five miles in your Aston Martin would use. And you'll probably enjoy those five miles in the Aston much more.

Tom: And if your wife is just testing you, well, so what? You're seventy-two. How much longer are you going to have to put up with the ramifications of failing the test? Not long! So now's the time, Michael. Send us a picture of you in the Aston, with the wind blowing through your bald spot.

HOW CAN I RUIN

DAD'S

MINIVAN?

The Perilous Intersection of Kids, Parents, and Cars

HOW CAN I RUIN DAD'S MINIVAN?

Dear Tom and Ray:

I'm a seventeen-year-old and I've listened to your radio show and read your column for many years. My dad has an old Dodge Caravan (I guess he must have been a nerd) with a five-speed transmission. My mom just bought a new car, so I usually get stuck driving his old van, which is embarrassing. The only good news is that it has 223,000 miles on it. It has the original clutch and it still works great. The stupid thing won't break. He taught me, my sister, and my sister's friend how to drive a stick on it, and the clutch won't die. I've even tried teaching my friends on it. When I drive it around I try to peel out because he said not to do it. It doesn't even slip. My question is, how can I ruin this car real bad, so he won't even want to get another one? Thanks.

—Neil

P.S. It would be great if I could make it look like an accident.

Tom: Well, you can let my seventeen-year-old son drive it. That seems to be the kiss of death for any car.

Ray: Neil, I think you're approaching this all wrong. You're looking for a mechanical solution to what is essentially an emotional problem.

Tom: Right. I mean, you can simply ride the clutch—leaving it halfway out while you drive around—and eventually it'll burn out. But your father will just replace it. It's a few hundred bucks, and what's that compared to the cost of a new car, right?

Ray: Or you could loosen up the drain plug and let all of the oil run out, causing the engine to seize. But then, if there's any justice in this world, he'll see this column, rebuild the engine, and take the money out of your allowance until you're thirty-eight!

Tom: So, I think a more clever—and less harmful—approach is called for. Try this, Neil. Say, "Hey, Dad, can I take your Caravan tonight? I love driving it because there's lots of room in the back for me and my girlfriend (wink, wink)."

Ray: I bet he'll say, "Oh no, mister. That Caravan stays home. You're taking your mother's brand new Miata, and I don't want to hear another word about it!"

THE COST OF SENDING A CAR TO COLLEGE

Dear Tom and Ray:

My daughter in college has a six-year-old Volkswagen Golf with about 50,000 miles. So far this year, we have replaced the heater core, both fuel pumps, a CV joint, the radio (partly her fault), the horn, the windshield-wiper motor, and the whole exhaust system. What will be next? Really! So far, the car and tuition are running neck and neck!

—Bob

Ray: Well, Bob, that sounds about right to us. There's a formula we use to determine the maintenance costs for a car driven by a child at college.

Tom: The equation is $M = C - ADP - (ADB \times 1.5) + GPA \times \frac{2}{SAT} + \frac{R}{S} + NFBHT$

Ray: So, to figure out what the maintenance costs (*M*) should be, take the cost of the car (*C*) minus the amount Daddy paid (*ADP*) minus the amount Daddy borrowed (*ADB*) times 1.5. Add in the kid's grade point average (*GPA*) times two, divided by her SAT scores. Then add the average number of relationships she has per semester ($\frac{R}{S}$) and the all-important number of friends she brings home for Thanksgiving (*NFBHT*).

Tom: So according to this formula, the next repair ought to cost you $217.59, and it'll probably be the brakes.

Ray: Actually, Bob, just try to think of this as part of a good liberal arts education. Aside from learning philosophy, history, and anthropology, your daughter's going to graduate with a great introduction to the fascinating world of parts and labor.

WORRIED ABOUT SON

Dear Tom and Ray:

Earlier this year, my wife and I bought a used Dodge Daytona for our son to drive. Although he considers himself a student athlete, he thinks it wise to drive the entire half mile to school. My contention is that this is one of the worst things he might do to an automobile, since the oil and exhaust system never get warmed up enough to evaporate out condensation. I say this shortens the life of the exhaust system and encourages the formation of sludge in the oil pan. And I believe that this is even worse in the winter. Although I realize it is not fashionable for a teenager to be seen walking to school, I have difficulty reconciling in my mind the images of a young man driving a half mile to school and then running several miles at track practice after school before driving a half mile back home. But I'm not asking for psychiatric help, just car advice. Is this bad for the car?

—Richard

Tom: Absolutely, Richard. And you're 100 percent right about why it's bad. You've hit the nail right on the head.

Ray: But I wouldn't worry too much about your son's car. He's probably driving all over town during his lunch period with four girls in the backseat.

Tom: And, out of respect for your feelings about short drives, he probably quit the track team two months ago and is spending two more hours driving around after school.

Ray: So, I'm sure the car is fine. I'm glad we were able to ease your mind, Richard. Don't hesitate to write again if anything else worries you.

TELL YOUR KID TO HOWL AT THE MOON

Dear Tom and Ray:

I've heard one of you guys wax eloquent about the trials and tribulations of having a nineteen-year-old son. I have one who's a sophomore in college. He chose a small liberal arts college because he wouldn't need a car there (and, therefore, I could afford the much higher tuition versus the state university). But now he finds he absolutely can't survive without a car. Seems like "bait and switch" to me. He's done some research, and he thinks a Jeep Wrangler would fit his bill perfectly. Any advice?

—*Charles*

Tom: Yeah. Tell him to go howl at the moon, Charles.

Ray: After careful consideration, I would have to agree with that approach.

Tom: First of all, we don't recommend Jeep Wranglers for kids. They're too easy to flip over if you drive them irresponsibly. And we all know that youth is a time when people are more likely to act irresponsibly. Except me. I was a perfect child.

Ray: Yeah. Ask any of his parole officers.

Tom: But more important, you should insist that this kid buy his own car, Charles. The college years are supposed to be sort of a transition from childhood to adulthood. And making tough choices is one of the things adults have to do.

Ray: So if he's really got the hots for a Jeep Wrangler, he might have to work in the dining hall a few nights a week instead of going out with his friends to see *Attack of the Killer Tomatoes*. Let it be his choice.

Tom: If he's like most kids, once he has to come up with the money himself, his expectations will come way down. And he'll probably end up with something like a 1978 Olds Cutlass Salon.

Ray: And that'll lead to other important life lessons . . . like how to use jumper cables and add transmission fluid!

DANGER: FIVE-YEAR-OLD WITH HOSE

Dear Tom and Ray:

Yesterday, during my biannual car washing, my five-year-old squirted water up the tailpipe. I did not see her do this, but I was alerted when she came around to the front and asked "Would it be OK to get that hole wet?" At my request for a reenactment—without the water—she said she put the hose nozzle up to the pipe and squeezed with both hands and, "Whoooosh! I did it a lot of times." I have a seven-year-old Mazda 626 with 150,000 miles, and it's the "good" car. Am I in trouble? I haven't driven it since then except for a ten-minute drive. I have a forty-mile commute tomorrow. Please advise.

—Judy

Tom: Don't worry about a thing, Judy. Since the car started, it's absolutely fine.

Ray: If you put enough water in there, I suppose it's possible to block the exhaust from coming out. Then you'd have the equivalent of a potato in the tailpipe, and the car wouldn't start. But that's tough to do, even for a determined five-year-old.

Tom: So what you had was a bunch of water in the tailpipe and muffler. And what happened is that when you started the car, the pressure in the exhaust system pushed most of it out, and the rest was vaporized by the heat and then sent out the tailpipe. The exhaust system gets up to several hundred degrees Fahrenheit when the motor's running. And that's enough to vaporize any remaining water in very short order.

Ray: If you had let the water sit in there for a week, that might have led to premature rusting of the muffler and tailpipe. But since you drove it right away, I don't think you have to worry at all.

Tom: And water is not a foreign substance in there, Judy. Water is one of the byproducts of a gasoline engine. So the exhaust system knows just what to do with this stuff. Tell your daughter that, next time, if she really wants you to spend more time at home with her, she needs to pack a bunch of pancake mix in there before adding the water.

BUT WHAT ABOUT MY BATTERY?

Dear Tom and Ray:

My son and his friends sometimes sit for an hour or two in my Mercury Grand Marquis. They sit with the motor off, listening to the radio with the key in the accessory position. They usually do this on Friday or Saturday evenings instead of coming inside and going to bed. Will listening to the car radio for two hours drain the battery? Should I chase them out of the car and tell them to go to the mall instead?

—Ed

Tom: Absolutely not! This is exactly where you want them. I'm sure there are parents out there who would love to know that their teenage kids are right out in the driveway listening to the radio, instead of doing who knows what. This is a blessing, Ed.

Ray: The battery will be fine. Unless you have one of those 5,000-watt master blasters—which we rarely see on Grand Marquis—they'd have to run the radio all night, and then some, to run down the battery to the point where the car wouldn't start.

Tom: And even if they did, say, accidentally leave it on all night and kill the battery, it wouldn't do any permanent damage. You wouldn't have to buy a new battery. You'd simply have to jump-start the car, and then drive around to charge it up. Once you did that, everything would be fine again.

Ray: But under no circumstances would I throw the boys out of the car. It's kind of charming that they like pretending they're older and driving around listening to the radio. And unlike in future years, there's an extremely low likelihood that they'll crack up your car while it's parked in the driveway, Ed. So enjoy these good old days while they last.

THE RULES FOR PUNCH BUGGY

Dear Tom and Ray:

My dad and I are having an argument about Punch Buggy. Today he saw an original Beetle. He punched me for it, but I said that the originals don't count. He says they do. We have agreed that you guys are to be the final judges in our dispute. So, do original Beetles count in Punch Buggy?

—Syd

Ray: Well, for those who are not familiar with Punch Buggy, it's a game that sadistic little kids developed while riding around with their parents several decades ago. The idea was that if you were the first one to see a Volkswagen Beetle on the road, you say, "Punch Buggy" and then punch your opponent in the arm.

Tom: This explains why my brother's left arm was swollen to roughly twice the size of his right arm during most of his childhood.

Ray: I think we'd have to conclude, with very little deliberation, Syd, that old, original VW Beetles certainly do count. They're the cars that started the whole Punch Buggy game, so how can you exclude them? They're getting quite rare these days, so you won't see many of them, but I don't think there's any question that they earn you a punch.

Tom: So tell your dad he's right, Syd. And then call Children's Protective Services and turn him in. That'll teach him to argue with you next time.

NEVER LISTEN TO YOUR BROTHER WHEN IT COMES TO CARS

Dear Tom and Ray:

I was trying to get into my dad's car, which was locked, and I didn't have the key. My younger brother told me to pick the lock. So I put a piece of wood in the lock, and it broke off. And now we can't use the key in the lock. My dad says I have to pay for someone to fix it unless I can figure out a way to get it out of there. Do you have any suggestions? I am thirteen and don't have a job, so I really need your help.

—Spencer

Tom: Oh, Spencer. I hope that at the very least you've learned one of life's most important lessons: Never listen to your younger brother about anything!

Ray: My brother's just still miffed about the time I convinced him that he could get rid of his zits by painting them with a laundry marker.

Tom: I'm not sure I really have any good ideas for you, Spencer. I assume you've tried to fit a pair of tweezers in there. But the key slot is really too small for you to be able to use them, even if they do go in.

Ray: Well, the solution is obvious to me: Fire. Wood burns, right? You need to stick a lit match in the keyhole and ignite the piece of wood. It'll burn up, turn to ash, and the problem will be solved.

Tom: Spencer, if you saw how mad your father was when he found out about the wood, just imagine how he's going to react when he finds his entire car burnt to a crisp. Don't listen to my brother, Spencer! He's a younger brother, remember?

Ray: All right, here's another idea. Get a long pin. Using needle-nose pliers, bend the tip of it 90 degrees. Then try to stick the end of the pin into the piece of wood, and fish it out that way. Or, you might try going to the drugstore and getting a dental tool that has a point on the end. If the shaft is thin enough, it'll be a stronger version of the pin tool.

Tom: Well, you can try it, Spencer, but I suspect, in the end, you're going to have to call a locksmith. It'll cost you $50, which you'll have to work off by mowing lawns.

Ray: Or just break into your father's wall safe and take the money. You can break in using a piece of wood, you know.

Tom: Spencer, go out and earn the money and get the lock fixed. And consider it a small price to pay for an important lesson about brotherly advice.

JERK OR GENIUS?

Dear Tom and Ray:

Am I a jerk or a genius? My son is now eighteen, and when he was fifteen, I wrote him a check for $1,500, postdated three years. I told him that if he managed to reach the date of the check without (1) receiving any tickets, (2) being involved in any accidents, or (3) breaking any of our house driving rules, I'd cash the check for him. My goal was to provide an incentive for him to play by the rules long enough to form some good driving habits. Anyway, my son very nearly made it. A few months shy of his eighteenth birthday, he received a speeding ticket. He was cruising along the highway, singing. And he suddenly realized that the light show accompanying his karaoke act was being provided by the flashing lights on top of a cruiser. He fessed up about the ticket promptly, and was bemoaning the fine of $126. I gently reminded him that the ticket had actually cost him $1,626, as he had failed to fulfill our bargain. My question: Am I a genius for coming up with the carrot that made him a good driver during his crucial first years behind the wheel, or am I a jerk for piling on a $1,500 fine? Please note that his younger sister is watching carefully to see how this is resolved. She's fourteen, and whether I fold on this will go a long way in setting her expectations. My son took the news well, but I have friends who are treating me as though I smashed the kid's piggy bank and took his inheritance. Your take on this ethical dilemma?

—Ted

Tom: Are you a jerk or a genius? Well, it's possible to be both, Ted. I'd say you're definitely a genius. I think this is a brilliant way to encourage a kid to drive responsibly, and I'm all for anything that accomplishes that.

Ray: I agree. Clearly it has worked. For nearly three years the kid was careful. He avoided getting tickets, he avoided accidents, and he lived by the rules of the household. Do you know how many insanely jealous parents are reading about this kid today?

Tom: So you definitely get points for parenting. Now, are you also a jerk? Actually, I don't think so. The fact that you're asking us whether you're a jerk means you're not one. Because jerks, by definition, never think they're being jerks. So clearly, you sense—somewhere in that hard, little, dried-up stone of a heart you have—that you're being a little rough on the kid.

Ray: I understand the desire to teach your kids that "a deal is a deal." But it's also worth teaching them about fairness, flexibility, and that there's value in trying hard, even if you don't always succeed. After all, your mission is essentially accomplished. After driving responsibly for his first three years, your son is unlikely to turn around now and go out and drive like a moron.

Tom: So, I would extend your offer. Make it clear to him—and to his younger sister—that since he dutifully fulfilled the contract for most of the three years, you appreciate his effort and you want to offer him a chance to redeem himself.

Ray: Right. Tell him that if he maintains a clean record for an additional six months after the original deadline, you'll still cash the check for him. Or you'll cash a slightly smaller check—say $1,400—for him. And you can make it clear to both kids that were it not for his excellent performance up until the speeding ticket, you wouldn't be offering him a second chance.

Tom: You can also make it clear that this is a one-time offer. That if he fails again, you intend to cash the check yourself and spend the money on that vibrating recliner you've had your eye on.

Ray: But you both deserve a lot of credit. You came up with a great idea, and your son has had the good sense to buy into the deal. Congratulations to both of you.

FORMER DELINQUENT REFORMED?

Dear Tom and Ray:

I've been a fan of yours for a long time, and I thought you might be able to help. When I was a kid growing up in the Bronx, I had a fascination with the emblems on VWs and used to steal them. They popped off easily with a screwdriver. I'm not proud of having done that, and my dad actually had to come get me at the police precinct after I was caught in a hospital parking lot trying to lift one of the emblems off a doctor's car. I'm now in my mid-fifties and would like to be able to purchase the emblems (without the cars attached) in order to re-create my adolescent collection. Any suggestions where to go?

—Bob

Tom: Well, you can buy them new, Bob. They're sold as replacement parts—mostly to VW owners who've had their emblems stolen by rotten little kids!

Ray: You can get those new ones from any local VW dealer, or find them for sale online from auto-parts stores that do business on the Internet.

Tom: But I suspect that what you really want are used VW emblems—ones that have a history, even if you don't know what that history is. And you probably want a bunch of different ones, from different-size VWs. You want a small one from a Jetta, and a big one from a Microbus.

Ray: You can find those on eBay. Most of them are being sold by rotten little kids who've popped them off VWs in hospital parking lots. Maybe if you threaten to turn the kid in, he'll confess to how he got it, and you'll be able to relive your entire youth vicariously. Good luck, Bob.

•*Massachusetts*• 08
CHPTR3

IT'S NOT A

PUPPY

Care and Feeding
of Your Car

IT'S NOT A PUPPY

Dear Tom and Ray:

I am an elderly woman, and I like to take very good care of my car. My question concerns a car that has to be left outside in the winter with no garage and is only used about once a week. Is it wise when the temperature drops below zero to go out and start the car and let it idle for a few minutes?

—Lucie

Tom: Second to letting my brother borrow it, Lucie, that is just about the worst thing you can do to that poor little car.

Ray: First of all, you may do damage to the engine by starting it. When you start the car in that kind of weather, it takes a few minutes for the oil to really heat up and thin out. And until it thins out, it can't properly lubricate the moving parts of the engine. So those first few minutes are very hard on your car. So you should avoid cold starts unless you're really going to drive.

Tom: Plus, if you just start the car in weather like that, and just let it idle for a few minutes, the engine won't heat up. And the carbon and moisture produced by the engine never get cleared out, which is also bad.

Ray: So if you don't need the car, just let it sit there. It's not like a little puppy out there in the cold. It's just an inanimate object. Trust us. It doesn't care.

Tom: Oh no, now we're going to get nasty mail again from PHARTIO: People for the Humane and Respectful Treatment of Inanimate Objects.

Ray: If you do need the car in extremely cold weather, here are some of the tips we give in our pamphlet "Ten Ways You May Be Ruining Your Car Without Even Knowing It" (which you can get by visiting the Shameless Commerce Division of our Web site, cartalk.com). First, don't step on the gas pedal as soon as the car shows signs of life. Remember, the oil is very thick when it's cold, and revving the engine before the oil has thinned out will do a lot of harm. If it wants to stall, let it stall. That's better than revving it to death.

Tom: Second, if possible, plan your driving so that you drive the car for at least half an hour. Remember, the engine needs to heat up in order to get rid of that moisture and soot it produces. So try to avoid just using the car for really short trips.

Ray: Of course, when it's minus-6 degrees outside, that's when you're most tempted to use the car to go two blocks for a quart of milk. But do yourself a favor and consider calling a cab in those situations. Besides, the cab will already be nice and toasty the minute you get into it.

READ ALL ABOUT IT!

Dear Tom and Ray:

I own a Saturn SL1 with 58,000 miles on it. It's a wonderful car that has very few problems, but I do have one concern. Periodically, my "Service Engine Soon" light comes on, stays on for a while, then blinks off. My oil is full and recently changed, and all the other fluid levels are full. What is causing this, and is it serious?

—Nikki

Ray: This light is telling you that a certain maintenance procedure is required right now, Nikki. We'll tell you how to do it.

Tom: Start by going out to your Saturn and unlocking the passenger door, not the driver's door. Then get in.

Ray: Right in front of you, you'll see the flip-down door to the glove compartment. Open it.

Tom: Now rummage through the gas-card receipts, the Sleepy LaBeef cassettes, and the pistachio shells, and reach down toward the bottom of the glove compartment.

Ray: If you feel around down there, you'll feel a flat, somewhat shiny object. Remove it.

Tom: That's the owner's manual. And the procedure you need to perform is to read it.

Ray: I realize it's not exactly a Michael Crichton thriller, but there's a lot of very useful information in there, including the answer to your question.

Tom: What you'll find is that the "Service Engine Soon" light is what many other cars call the "Check Engine" light. It's not an emergency, but it means that one of the signals going into the computer is not reading what it's supposed to be reading.

Ray: And the reason could be anything from a bad sensor to a bona fide engine problem. Your mechanic will be able to tap into the computer and read the "trouble code" on his scanner and figure out what it is. That's why it says "Service Engine Soon."

Tom: I think they changed the name because when the "Check Engine" light came on, people like my brother would get out, check the engine, and if the engine was still there, they'd get back in the car and drive away. So I guess "Service Engine Soon" is for people who took the "Check Engine" light too literally.

THE CHEAPSKATE'S DILEMMA

Dear Tom and Ray:

I have a Toyota Tercel that has never given me a moment's trouble. I have more than 100,000 miles on it, and I've never even had it serviced. Risky, I know, but in retrospect, nothing has ever gone wrong! Until now. The brakes are gone. The least-expensive estimate is $500 for all four wheels. Here's my question: How easy would it be for me, a woman, to fix the brakes myself (with help with the muscle work from my husband, who, incidentally, has replaced his love of horsepower with a love of RAM)? I know my way around cars a bit. I have installed an in-line fuel filter on a '76 Nova and replaced thermostats in cars ranging from a Willys Jeep to a Pontiac Grand Prix. I have never fixed brakes, though. I'd like to save the labor charges. Should I try it?

—Bede

Tom: Bede, I would guess from your question that you are an absolute, world-class cheapskate. Am I right?

Ray: This, from a man who would reuse his toothpaste if it were possible to separate it from his spit.

Tom: Seriously, Bede. You've gone 100,000 miles and haven't spent a penny on this car. Now, the most important safety feature on the car—the brakes—are shot, endangering you and everybody you drive past on the road, and your biggest concern is saving a few bucks?

Ray: I'd have to agree. While it's not impossible for you to do it, a complete brake job (pads, rotors, possibly calipers) on a modern car is a significant step up, mechanically, from throwing a fuel filter in a '76 Nova. And, more important, the stakes are a lot higher.

Tom: Right. If you screw up the fuel filter, the worst that will happen is that the car won't start. If the brakes don't work, the car won't stop! It's just not the kind of job you want to do for the first time unsupervised.

Ray: So you should just swallow your pride and pay a trained mechanic the $500 to do the brake job professionally. And do it immediately. If your brakes really are completely "gone"—and they probably are after 100,000 miles—you may be the next thing to go!

EXPERTS AGREE: DRIVING WITHOUT OIL IS A LOUSY IDEA

Dear Tom and Ray:

My son took his ten-year-old car in for an oil change yesterday and they forgot to refill it with oil. He drove it about five miles before it quit on him. He pulled into a parking lot and called me for help. I asked him to check the dipstick, and it read empty. We had it towed back to the shop and they filled it with oil, drained it again, and then refilled it again with oil. They then took it to another garage, which checked it over and said everything sounded fine. Do you think any damage was done?

—Neil

Ray: Probably. Most experts agree that one should not run a car without oil in it. And the fact that it died on him while he was driving indicates that it started to seize up and probably did damage the rings and the bearings.

Tom: His mistake was stopping. If he had just kept on driving until the engine was absolutely cooked, there would have been no question about the fact that they owe you an engine. But since it's still running, they can have their buddies at the other shop give it the thumbs up and send you on your way. Then they just have to hope that by the time the car starts burning a quart of oil every fifty miles, either (A) your son will be living in a different state, or (B) they will have been abducted by aliens or the Better Business Bureau.

Ray: I'd tell them that you want to have the car checked out independently before you let them off the hook. Have a mechanic of your choosing do an oil leak-down test. And, if necessary, have him remove the oil pan and visually inspect the bearings. He may see that the bearings actually are burned.

Tom: And if that's the case, you'll just have to press them to share the cost of fixing it. They won't pay for a new engine—nor should they, really—because the engine you drove in with was at least ten years old. But they should pay for a portion of the rebuilding cost, or they should buy you a used engine and install it. You'll have to negotiate with their insurance company.

Ray: All decent shops carry insurance to cover bonehead maneuvers like this. It's part of the cost of being in the auto-repair business. And if they employ anyone like my brother, I'm sure they've opted for the lowest-possible deductible. So don't feel bad about pushing this, Neil. It was their mistake.

WHAT A MESS!

Dear Tom and Ray:

I am the proud owner of two vehicles with horizontally mounted filters. Both of them are Fords—a big Bronco and an Escort wagon. Do you have any tips for removing these oil filters without creating a mess? Letting the engine drain a long time before removing the filter helps some, but who can wait 24 hours for the oil to drain? I've tried prewrapping the filter with a plastic bag or newspaper, I've tried hanging funnels, and most recently, I intentionally punctured the filter to allow it to drain into a cup before removing it. My results: a worse mess! This never happened on my previous cars whose filters hung down at a 45-degree angle. Do you know the answer to changing these filters without ending up with oil all over me?

—Phillip

Tom: Sure. The answer is your local gas station or Quickie Lube, Phillip. Research clearly shows that if you stand in the waiting room, the mess—at least from your point of view—is reduced significantly.

Ray: There is no good answer, Phillip. We make a mess when we change these types of filters, too. We use a huge drain bucket that's about 2½ feet in diameter, and that catches most of it.

Tom: And you can buy a drain bucket like that yourself at your local auto parts store. It's actually a transmission oil drain bucket, and it's designed to catch oil dripping from a large transmission oil pan.

Ray: But even that won't get all of it. Some of the oil will still run down the side of the engine and keep dripping long after you've cleaned up and gone in for dinner.

Tom: So I guess the only way to eliminate 100 percent of the mess is to have it done by somebody else. Or do what I do. I use the transmission fluid drain bucket, and I do all my work in my brother's driveway.

BORROWED TIME

Dear Tom and Ray:

I need your advice. I have a 1991 Nissan Maxima with 69,000 miles. The dealer tells me I'm driving on borrowed time by not having the timing belt changed. The guys at my office think I'm nuts for even considering such a thing when the car is running fine. I have yet to talk to anyone who has replaced a timing belt as preventive maintenance.

—Debbie

Ray: Until now! I've replaced timing belts as preventive maintenance a jillion times.

Tom: How many is a jillion? Is that one more zero than a bazillion?

Ray: We recommend that all our customers change their timing belts at their manufacturer's recommended interval. Check your owner's manual to find out what's advised for your car. It's usually between 60,000 and 110,000 miles. In your case, the recommendation is 60,000 miles.

Tom: There are two good reasons to change your timing belt. Reason No.1 is that when the timing belt breaks, the car stops running. And that can be inconvenient if you happen to be a quarter of a jillion miles from home when it breaks.

Ray: But the other reason is that some cars have engines that are designed in such a way that when the timing belt breaks, the valves get crushed, and sometimes the entire engine gets ruined. And guess what, Debbie? You've got one of those cars!

Tom: Right. Nissans and Hondas of this era fall into that "motor wrecker" category, among others. So, for you, it's especially important that you change the belt at 60,000 miles—or in your case, 69,001 (i.e., as soon as possible). It'll cost you around $300 to replace the belt. But that's nothing compared to the $2.6 bazillion you'll spend on a new engine if the timing belt breaks before you get to it.

TO DOWNSHIFT OR NOT TO DOWNSHIFT? THAT IS THE QUESTION.

Dear Tom and Ray:

I have the great misfortune of having a know-it-all friend. I drive a Toyota Corolla, and he drives a Corvette. While visiting him, I found myself being chastised for downshifting. His argument was that "Click and Clack said not to downshift." A short time later, I heard you two guys advising a sweet young lady to downshift. What's the story?

—John

Ray: Well, John, as my mother used to say to me whenever I put a broken transmission on the kitchen table just before dinner, "There's a time and a place for everything."

Tom: When we tell people not to downshift, we're talking about downshifting on normal roads during everyday driving. I'm sure your friend in the Corvette—before he heard our advice—used to downshift into second as he approached every red light. Why? Because he thought he was "saving the brakes." But more important, because it sounded cool and he was trying to get girls to turn their heads and notice him.

Ray: But at some point, he probably heard us explain that he was ruining his clutch by downshifting so often. And two or three clutches later, he started to believe us.

Tom: On the other hand, there is one situation in which you absolutely do want to downshift and save the brakes. And that's when you're going down a long, steep hill. If, for example, you're coming down a mountain road and you constantly use the brakes, you're liable to overheat them. And if they overheat, the brake fluid can boil. And if that happens, you'll find yourself at the bottom of the mountain much more quickly than you would have expected!

Ray: So on a long, steep hill, you *should* put your manual or automatic transmission in a gear low enough to keep you at a safe, comfortable speed. If the hill is so steep that you're still speeding up and having to ride the brakes, drop it a gear lower and try again.

Tom: And if you're really lucky, there will be some girls walking up the mountain who will turn their heads and notice you.

YOU DON'T SEE COWS USING ARMOR ALL

Dear Tom and Ray:

I just bought a Ford Explorer with leather seats. Since this is my first time owning leather seats, I'd like to know if there are any special techniques to care for my leather upholstery. I ask this question because the leather upholstery in my parents' car is cracked and well worn. I would like to keep my new seats looking their best for as long as possible. Any suggestions?

—Michelle

Tom: Well, if you're really determined to keep your seats looking new as long as possible, you can use the time-honored method that every immigrant American household has used, which is to cover the things up with plastic.

Ray: Right. My grandmother plastic-covered every piece of furniture she ever bought. The nicer the furniture, the thicker the plastic. And it worked. When she died, her furniture looked great.

Tom: Of course, the plastic was also responsible for her demise. She stuck to her couch one hot, humid day in August, and we didn't find her until a week later.

Ray: Actually, there's not much you have to do with leather. That's its great advantage. I mean, you don't see cows wiping each other down with Armor All out in the pasture, do you?

Tom: The cracking is the result of the leather drying out. And depending on the climate you live in and how much sun beats into the car every day, you may want to treat the leather seats with a leather conditioner every six months or so as a precaution. A number of companies make leather conditioners—just check any auto-parts store or the automotive section of a department store. The conditioner's purpose is to moisturize the leather and keep it from drying out and cracking. Other than that, all you have to do is wash it with some mild soap and warm water once in a while, and it should last the life of the car.

Ray: Oh, I do have one other suggestion. Get out of the habit of keeping your uncovered ballpoint pen in your back pocket.

MY BABY . . . SHE'S GONE!

Dear Tom and Ray:

I cry as I write. My baby—my Mazda Miata, with 28,800 miles, was stolen ten days ago. I had an alarm. At 2 A.M., a neighbor heard an alarm go off, then it was disarmed. Then, five to ten minutes later, it went off again and the tires squealed. I'm in an apartment with a carport only, no garage, no iron gates, and no security guard. I plan to replace the car with another Miata. My question is, what type of antitheft device do you recommend?

—Debbie

Tom: The best alarm system in the world, Debbie, is a large, surly German shepherd. Because the only way you can defeat it is with a large bucket of extra-crispy KFC chicken wings.

Ray: Of course, in a Miata, a dog that size may create some window-fogging problems for you.

Tom: Actually, you've corroborated our theory that car alarms are totally useless. Your neighbor heard the alarm and didn't do anything. Why? Either he figured there was a potentially dangerous car thief down there and he didn't want to get bopped on the head or worse, or, more likely, he figured, "It's another annoying false alarm, and some moron's car theft system is malfunctioning again." Either way, it didn't do anything to save your Miata, did it?

Ray: In my opinion, the most effective antitheft device is one that prevents the thief from ever starting the car. And I would recommend a hidden switch that kills the power to the ignition, the fuel pump, or both. Have your mechanic hide a switch for you. Don't use one of the standard switches that all professional thieves know about now, like blinker switch up, lights on, window up, etc.

Tom: If you have a switch that's not in an obvious place, then if a thief tries to steal your car, it'll crank and crank but never start. And believe me, if he can't find a kill switch, no thief is going to take the time to diagnose the problem and figure out why the car isn't starting. And if he does figure it out, you should let us know, because we could use a few good mechanics at our garage.

Ray: Of course, if you don't want to install some sort of kill switch, you can always use my brother's theft deterrent. He drives a car nobody else would ever want: a '63 Dodge Dart. And as an added deterrent, he's let the smell inside the car get so bad that even if a thief could bear to sit in it long enough to start it, he'd never survive the getaway.

MOTOR HONEY FOR YOUR

CHARIOT

Myths, Gimmicks, Quacks, and Other Automotive Skulduggery

MOTOR HONEY FOR YOUR CHARIOT

Dear Tom and Ray:

My daughter has an old Chevy Nova, which is using about two quarts of oil a week. The car is being driven less than 200 miles a week and now has 89,000 miles on it. She recently replaced the timing belt, the clutch and clutch master cylinder, the water pump, the fuel pump, and the head gasket. We've also had the cylinder head repaired, and many other parts changed. Prior to having all this work done, the Nova used five to eight quarts of oil a year, and shortly after this work, it started using two quarts a week. In your opinion, could any of this repair work have caused the problem? Could some part have been left out or some faulty adjustment have been made? My daughter would like to trade this car in, but with smoke pouring out the exhaust, she won't recover what she paid to have it repaired. Do you know of any additive we could use to lessen the smoke exhausted or the oil being consumed?

—James

Tom: Yeah, we know of an additive that will stop the smoke, James. Dollar bills. About 1,500 of them.

Ray: My guess is that you needed a head gasket and cylinder head job recently because the car overheated. And I suspect that when it overheated, your daughter kept right on driving anyway. That ruined not only the gasket and head, but probably the pistons, rings, and cylinder walls, too. And the only thing that will fix it is an engine rebuild.

Tom: I can sympathize with your request, James. I mean, since the time of the Pharaohs, people have been looking for a magical additive that would stop an engine from burning oil. It's a little known fact that when they opened up the pyramids in Egypt, in addition to the bodies of the Pharaohs, they also found hundreds of empty bottles of "motor honey."

Ray: Your daughter has to decide how much she likes this car, James. If she's willing to drive it a few more years, then spend $1,500 and rebuild the engine. At least you know you won't need a clutch or fuel pump, right?

Tom: And if she's really determined to get rid of it, then swallow hard, stuff a couple bananas in the crankcase, and see what the dealer will give you for it. Good luck.

A BATTERY BUDDY FOR BONEHEADS

Dear Tom and Ray:

I have a bad habit of parking the car with the lights on once or twice a year and draining the battery. Our Toyota Corolla does not have a system for turning off the lights in cases like that. Recently, I saw an ad for a device called the Battery Brain that claims to rescue people like me from their absentmindedness. The device measures the output of the battery, and if the voltage drops below a certain number of volts, it automatically switches off all battery discharge to save the remaining power to start the car. When you get back to the car, you have to open the hood and press the reset button, but at least you'll be able to start the car. What do you think of this thing?

—Roger

Ray: We've never tried one, but doesn't sound like a bad idea, Roger. If you know you're a bonehead—like my brother—then it makes perfect sense to take steps to protect yourself.

Tom: Don't be ashamed, Roger. Some people, like you and me, just have more important things to think about than turning off our lights. We're busy solving the world's problems, trying to make peace between the Red Sox and Yankees fans, trying to invent clean-burning pollution-free fuel cells, trying to predict tonight's winning lottery number.

Ray: Most people don't leave their lights on often enough to justify a $50 expenditure on a box like this. But if it's worth it to you, then go for it. And let us know how well it works. Just make sure you know how to disconnect it. If it were ever to malfunction or fail to reset, the device itself could keep you from starting the car.

Tom: And in that case, you'll want to be able to remove it promptly . . . and stomp on it until it breaks into little tiny pieces.

PLEASE DON'T SQUEEZE THE OIL FILTER

Dear Tom and Ray:

While I was attending the University of Oklahoma in 1960, a study was done by the petroleum engineering department. The question was: Is draining oil from a vehicle necessary? They worked with White Trucking Company and tested their theory on long-haul trucks. Using only a toilet paper filter and only adding oil, they ran one set of trucks against ones that received oil and filter changes for 100,000 miles. The results showed no significant wear differences between the two. They also concluded that the oil in the no-change vehicle was stronger, because the weak molecules in the oil broke down and evaporated away. This study was going on at about the time that the Conoco Oil company was working on biofuel and had developed a plant in Bartlesville, Oklahoma. But then both the study and the plant were suddenly gone, and I never heard any more. What is your take on the oil-change theory?

—Don

Tom: Ah, yes. I remember that study, Don. It was funded by Charmin.

Ray: Actually, while we don't know anything about that particular study, I'd take it with a grain of salt.

Tom: First of all, motor oil has improved dramatically in the past fifty years. So whatever was done then probably doesn't apply now.

Ray: Also, long-haul diesel truck engines are built to last much longer than automobile engines. So 100,000 miles might not have been enough to show the damage of forgoing oil changes.

Tom: We have heard about the toilet-paper filter, though. It's called a Frantz Filter, and it has had a small cult following throughout the years. As you might expect, you install the housing, and then you simply stick a roll of 1,000-sheet, two-ply, 100-grit toilet paper in the holder, and that does the filtering. When it's dirty, you remove it and insert another roll.

Ray: It's not a surprise to us that it never caught on in big numbers, because it requires men to change a roll of toilet paper.

Tom: Aside from that fatal flaw, we've had good reports about it from our customers during the years. But keep in mind that anyone who would go through the trouble of installing and using one of these things obviously is very interested in car care and maintenance. That kind of person probably tends to take particularly good care of his car in all kinds of other ways, which could skew the results.

Ray: In any case, Don, our personal experience at the garage suggests that changing the oil and filter regularly is good, and not changing the oil and filter regularly can be very bad—even catastrophic—over the long haul.

Tom: And it's relatively cheap insurance. It's $20 or $30 a few times a year, for most people. So we still strongly believe in changing the oil in your car and changing the toilet-paper roll in the bathroom. And not vice versa.

ADIOS, RUSTY JONES. (AND YOU, TOO, ZIEBART.)

Dear Tom and Ray:

My wife and I are in the process of purchasing a brand-new minivan. Our question revolves around the issue of undercoating and rustproofing. Do we really need to have our car rustproofed? And if we do, who should we get to do it?

—Bob

Tom: We've stopped recommending rustproofing, Bob, for two reasons.

Ray: The lesser of the reasons is that manufacturers have improved their rust protection to some degree. They now dip the car parts in some sort of lactose-free, magnesium-zinc, corn syrup–based fruit shortening, which supposedly adds some protection against rusting.

Tom: And their "rust-through" corrosion guarantees reflect an increased confidence on their part that they've been at least somewhat successful—either in rustproofing their cars, or crafting warranty language that's vague enough to be weaseled out of easily.

Ray: The more important reason we don't recommend rustproofing is that it's usually done so badly that it actually makes the car more likely to rust, not less.

Tom: Let's face it, the guys that do the rustproofing are not recent graduates of the Starfleet Academy. And they're poking holes in the bottom of your brand-new car and supposedly squirting chemicals in door panels and body panels. And if they do it right, it can help your car last longer. But if they do a sloppy or incomplete job, one of two things can happen. If they don't put the chemicals where they're supposed to go, you can end up with extra holes, which can let moisture into the door and body panels and facilitate rusting. Or, if they put too much of the stuff in, your drain holes can get plugged up, which also accelerates the rusting process.

Ray: Now I'm sure the Continental Rustproofers United in Defense (CRUD) is going to be all over us for expressing such a blanket opinion. And I'm sure that there are some skilled, honest rustproofers out there. The problem is, even we don't know how to identify the good ones. If I bought a brand-new car tomorrow, I wouldn't know who I could trust to rustproof it correctly. And I'm in the automotive business—you know, honor among thieves and all that.

Tom: So unless you personally know and trust someone who rustproofs cars, our advice these days would be to keep the car clean and take your chances.

EXPLODING MYTHS

Dear Tom and Ray:

My wife drives 15 minutes to work five days a week. After a recent vacation when she didn't drive the car for a few weeks, I found the battery dead. I took the battery out and trotted up to the local service station, which shall remain nameless. I say this because the man wearing the star took my battery, put it on the bare concrete floor where the charger was, and connected the charging cables. A heated discussion proceeded between the two of us about the lack of a piece of wood for insulation between the battery and the floor. I have taken enough mechanic classes in my life now to remember being cautioned to never place a battery that you wanted to use again on the ground. Be it dirt or concrete, the battery's life would be shortened. Being told that it had something to do with the earth's mass being negatively charged was always enough for me to accept this rule of thumb. But the star man told me I was a fool for believing this absurd and unproven concept. What is your learned opinion? I'm on the verge of losing sleep over this issue.

—Ballan

Tom: I actually see two issues we need to address, Ballan. One is why it's okay to leave a car battery on a concrete floor, and the other is how you're going to apologize to this gas-station mechanic whose mother you probably insulted during this argument.

Ray: While there used to be some basis for not leaving a battery on the floor, it doesn't really apply anymore.

Tom: If the outside of a battery is covered with acid—on the sides and the bottom—then the moisture in the concrete (or in moist dirt, I suppose) could serve as a conductor, and could increase the rate at which the battery drains.

Ray: But even at that, you wouldn't expect to see any real change in the battery's effectiveness for many weeks.

Tom: Moreover, you just don't see batteries covered in acid these days, because most batteries are maintenance free, and they're sealed up pretty tight.

Ray: The only way you could make that kind of mess on a maintenance-free battery would be to severely overcharge it and make the acid bubble over onto the casing.

Tom: So this "rule" about leaving batteries on the floor made a small amount of sense before maintenance-free batteries, but it hardly applies anymore. In fact, a battery manufacturer near us says that during the summer they store their new batteries on the concrete floor because it keeps them cooler and therefore helps preserve their charge.

Ray: Now let's address the second issue—how you're going to prevent this guy at the local gas station from pouring Mountain Dew in your gas tank next time you come in. We know you told him in no uncertain terms what a stupid moron he is, and now you need an elegant way to back down.

Tom: Here's what you do: Tell him you didn't want the battery on the floor because you were afraid he might trip over it and hurt himself, and you were only looking out for his best interests. Good luck, Ballan.

NO TANKS FOR THE OIL

Dear Tom and Ray:

I feel stupid asking you this question, but I think my husband is nuts. He tells me to put oil into the gas tank of our 1980 Chevette. He says this will make it run better, but every time I do it, the car smokes and backfires. Please tell my husband that I'm right.

—Carrie

Tom: Well, Carrie, this is one of those good news, bad news situations. The good news is that you're absolutely right.

Ray: The bad news is what you're right about—your husband is indeed nuts. For decades, people have been adding things like Marvel Mystery Oil to their gasoline. No one knows exactly what it does; I guess that's why it's called "mystery" oil.

Tom: Actually, it's a "top-end lubricant." That's a lightweight oil designed to coat the upper parts of the engine—the intake valves in particular. What your husband is doing is using motor oil as a top-end lubricant. And as you can tell from all the smoke and backfiring, motor oil is much too heavy for that purpose. Basically you're making your car run like it burns a lot of oil.

Ray: But we should at least consider the possibility that your husband is not a complete nut, Carrie. Maybe he's finally coming to his senses and getting sick and tired of driving a car that represented the height of American automotive mediocrity the day it rolled off the assembly line nearly thirty years ago. Maybe he's secretly hoping to kill this car, and who are we to stand in the way? Or maybe he's embarrassed to have the only Chevette in town that isn't burning oil. He may just be showing his compassion—making the car backfire and belch blue smoke just so all the other Chevette owners won't feel so bad. What a nice guy, huh?

JUMP STARTS TIRE YOUR BATTERY

Dear Tom and Ray:

My loser friend keeps asking me to jump-start his loser car. I've done it about five times now, and I'm about ready to tell him where he can put his jumper cables. Is my battery going to suffer from all of this jump-starting? My Honda Civic is three years old and I haven't had to replace the battery yet, but I'm starting to worry. Is there some technical, car-lingo-laden excuse I can give him as to why I can't help him out next time his junk heap dies?

—Brad

Ray: Unfortunately, no, Brad. Jump-starting someone else's car is just like donating a pint of blood. A few days later, you'd never know it happened.

Tom: It's just like starting your own car one more time. So it hardly makes a difference in the life of your battery.

Ray: That doesn't mean we can't help you, though, Brad. If he's outworn his welcome, we'll be happy to help you make up a technical-sounding excuse.

Tom: Tell him that electron drainage during a jump start is magnified by Avogadro's number, and the tie-in between Coulomb's Law and the Heisenberg Uncertainty Principle makes it unwise to perform any more than five jump starts in a given year. Then throw in some reference to global warming and violations of the Southeast Asian Treaty Organization, and he should get the idea.

Ray: Or just tell him you're watching *Buffy the Vampire Slayer* and he should check the Yellow Pages under "AAA."

MORE MISERY
THANKS MISER

Dear Tom and Ray:

I saw a banner ad on a Web site (not yours) for a product called FuelMiser. This is a magnetic device that is attached to the fuel line and supposedly conditions the fuel to make it burn more efficiently. I read on and on about the science of how it works. I'm not an engineer, but the idea of the hydrocarbons being magnetically straightened out moments before they get burned sounded a bit dubious. On the other hand, spending $50 to achieve a 10 to 20 percent increase in fuel economy and decrease smog at the same time sounds great to me. But I would certainly like some independent validation of these claims. Your esteemed opinions, please?

—John

Ray: There's a certain trick to selling stuff like this, John. First, you have to have a somewhat believable scientific theory upon which to base your product. And these guys have that.

Tom: They claim that the molecules of gasoline are not ideally organized when they come down the fuel line. And that their magnet organizes the H's and C's so they burn more efficiently.

Ray: And you've never seen molecules of gasoline, right? So what do you know about how they're organized? They might live in group houses, for all you know. So it sounds pretty good, right?

Tom: And then you need to have the proper numbers. The right price used to be $19.95. But with inflation, it's now $49.95. That's the amount a person can spend without consulting a spouse. Or giving up HBO. It's a price at which you say, "Well, even if it doesn't work, it's not the end of the world."

Ray: Then you need the right "performance" numbers. Ten percent to 20 percent improvement is the proper range. If they promised to double your mileage, you'd know it was bull. But 10 or 15 percent? Sure, you can buy that.

Tom: It's also a number you can achieve through the placebo effect. In other words, after you install this thing, you follow the other "gas-saving tips" that come in the box—like accelerating gently, driving slower, taking the bus, and not warming up your car—and lo and behold, your mileage gets a little better.

Ray: You might have figured out by now, John, that we think this thing is a complete waste of money. I actually tried one in my truck, and I didn't notice any difference in mileage.

Tom: But he did, however, have a new place to store his paper clips—on the magnet under the hood—so it wasn't a total loss.

THE FIRST SPARK PLUG

ON THE MOON

Curious Car Conundrums

THE FIRST SPARK PLUG ON THE MOON

Dear Tom and Ray:

I was driving home from a friend's house and was on my way up a hill when I stopped at a stop sign. After restarting and letting the clutch out on my old Ford Escort GT with 120,000 miles on it, the peace was shattered by the sound of my No. 2 spark plug attempting to be the first such automotive part to land on the surface of the moon. It just blew right out of the engine with an incredibly loud noise. I found the plug lodged in the insulation on the underside of my hood. So I removed the fuzz, screwed the plug back into the block, and reattached the wire. After that, the car ran fine. Do I need to do anything else? And is this a sign that the end is near for this engine, or did my mechanic just forget to tighten this plug during my last tune-up?

—Randy

Tom: Isn't it amazing how much power spark plugs have when they shoot out of a cylinder like that? I've got about six bumps on my head from similar spark-plug launchings.

Ray: You mean the spark plugs blew out and hit you right in the head?

Tom: No, in each case, I was napping on the creeper underneath some other car, and the noise jolted me awake and caused me to bump my head on the transmission.

Ray: Your mechanic just forgot to tighten the plug, Randy. He screwed it in with his fingers and forgot to tighten it the rest of the way with the ratchet wrench. And as you drove around, the "explosions" in that cylinder slowly unscrewed the plug the rest of the way until finally it went kablooey. This is just one good reason why cars have a device called "the hood."

Tom: And as long as the plug wasn't damaged, you should be able to just screw it back in and keep driving. But there is one other thing you should do—check the other plugs to make sure they're tight.

Ray: There are torque (tightness) specifications for the plugs, and to be sure this doesn't happen again, you want to be sure all of your plugs are tightened to those specs. And always remember to drive with the hood closed.

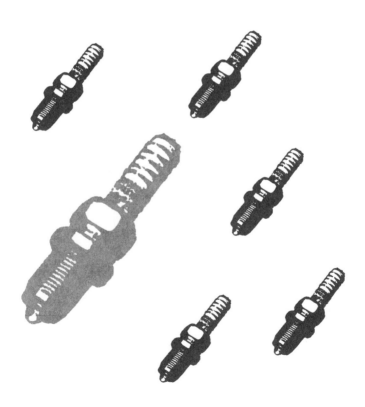

RADIATOR HOSE MAKES ULTIMATE SACRIFICE

Dear Tom and Ray:

We have three vehicles, which are parked in our driveway (we don't have a garage). Rats have hit them pretty hard. I've had to replace the main radiator hose on my Subaru Forester three times in just a few days. My van is now in the shop for numerous hoses and wiring damage. Someone suggested putting mothballs in the engine compartment, which I did. But a rat gnawed a huge hole in the radiator hose, right next to the mothballs. I have a pest guy coming, and I'm sure he'll reduce the local rat population, but I'm worried that my vehicles will eventually get hit again. Any suggestions?

—*Jim*

Ray: Well, you obviously didn't follow the instructions with the mothballs, Jim. You're supposed to put a big sign next to them that says, "You see what we did to the moths? Well, you guys are next."

Tom: We don't know much about rats, Jim, except that they're persistent . . . and adaptable . . . and they multiply like crazy. So I think you did the right thing by calling a professional. He'll undoubtedly look around and tell you if there are environmental factors at work, like construction nearby or loose garbage.

Ray: But if there's nothing that's specifically attracting them to your neighborhood or displacing them from their homes nearby, then the pest control probably will be only temporary.

Tom: So what do you do? You need some sort of early warning system. Something to let you know when the rats are back for more radiator snacks.

Ray: I've got it! You know how water heaters have "sacrificial anodes"—pieces of metal that "give themselves up" and rust so that the water heater itself doesn't rust? Well, Jim needs sacrificial radiator hoses.

Tom: Of course! Jim, you need to go to the junkyard and buy 100 old radiator hoses. Then lay them in a circle around all three cars. It'll be like a radiator-hose moat.

Ray: Right. And always park inside the moat. Then when you start to see the "early warning hoses" getting gnawed on, you'll know it's time to call the pest-control guy again. I love it.

Tom: Me, too. I have only one question: Is there even the remotest chance it'll work?

Ray: I don't know. Jim, write back and let us know. We have tons of extra radiator hoses lying around, and if we can repackage them as pest-control devices, it might be our ticket outta this dump!

LITTLE OLD LADY FROM GASOLINA

Dear Tom and Ray:

My Pontiac LeMans with 60,000 miles on it has a gasoline smell that comes into the car when I turn on the air-conditioner. I have smelled it outside the car for some time, but until recently I never smelled it inside. My mechanic says he cannot find anything, but I know it's there. Not only does it bother my sensitive nostrils, but I feel I always smell of gasoline when I get out of the car. I'm a little gray-haired old lady who has been helped by many of your columns over the years. I hope you can help me again now.

—Geraldine

Ray: We'd be delighted to help you, Geraldine. And we'll start with a little moral support. Even though your mechanic is trying to convince you that there's nothing wrong, I'm sure you do have a gasoline leak. You say you smell it, and I believe you.

Tom: Me, too. Obviously, a guy who spends all day with his head up under an engine is not going to be that sensitive to the smell of gasoline. If fact, if you think you smell bad, Geraldine, you ought to get a whiff of him!

Ray: The trick is finding the leak. Years ago, when we first opened our garage, it was a very difficult thing to do. I had to hold my brother by his feet and stick him, face-first, into the engine compartment so he could sniff around. But after he burned his nose on a hot exhaust manifold for the fifteenth or sixteenth time, he turned into a real crybaby about it.

Tom: That's when we started using our emissions tester to find gas leaks. And that's what your mechanic should do. The emissions tester is designed to detect unburned hydrocarbons (which is what gasoline is) in the exhaust. But there's no reason you can't use it to "sniff out" unburned gasoline under the hood, too.

Ray: Have your mechanic poke around the engine compartment with the emission tester's probe. When he sees the levels of hydrocarbons shoot up, he'll know he found the leak.

Tom: And get it fixed, Geraldine. I'm sure everyone in your bridge club is talking about "that horrible new fragrance Geraldine is wearing."

TEACHING AN OLD EL CAMINO NEW TRICKS

Dear Tom and Ray:

Have you ever had to "re-teach" a car to do something it forgot how to do? Surprisingly enough, it happened to me, and all it required was time and patience. I have a 1987 El Camino. About a month ago, the small green arrow light for the right turn indicator on the dashboard would go on, but it wouldn't blink. It would just stay on. During the past month, I gave the car "lessons" as to how it's supposed to work by manually flipping the right turn lever on and off repeatedly as a signal to drivers behind me. Lo and behold, four days ago, my indicator light has relearned how it is supposed to work and the problem is solved! Now it works perfectly. Patience is a strong virtue. One for the books.

—Maurice

Tom: This is how religions get started, Maurice. Some miraculous, unexplained event happens to some virtuous person, and before you know it, you've got scores of devoted followers. I can see it generations from now—El Camino owners all over the world sitting down once a year to retell the story of Maurice and the founding of Blinkerism!

Ray: Actually, there's a less spiritual explanation for this phenomenon, Maurice. The dashboard indicator light stays on when the circuit is not being completed—due to either a bad bulb, a loose or corroded connection, or a bad directional flasher. If I had to guess, given the miraculous recovery, I'd have to say you have a broken filament in one of the bulbs on the right side.

Tom: And rather than relearning how to blink, my guess is your filament got jolted back into place when you went over a bump four days ago. And if I'm right, some future bump will knock it out again and your problem will return.

Ray: When the problem does return, Maurice, put on the right blinker and get out and look at your front and rear turn-signal lights. One of them won't be on. If you replace that bulb (or fix the corroded connection to that bulb), the indicator light on your dash should blink for many years to come.

Tom: But just in case this "teaching" theory does have some validity, I've been sitting in my '63 Dodge Dart every morning saying, "Vrooom, vrooom," hoping my engine catches on to what it's supposed to be doing.

SATURN'S RINGS

Dear Tom and Ray:

Two weeks ago, I was putting a quart of oil into my Saturn SL. Much to my horror, the little plastic ring that's supposed to stay on the bottle after you twist off the cap fell into the engine. It floated down into the engine before I could fish it out. I've driven it since then. How much damage do you think I'll do if I keep driving it? Any advice, other than to sell the car quickly?

—Brenda

Tom: Brenda, we're sorry for not answering your question more quickly, but it was accidentally forwarded to the newspaper's astronomy columnist. I guess he automatically gets all the questions regarding rings floating around Saturns.

Ray: That was bad.

Tom: I know. And I apologize.

Ray: Selling it is a little drastic, Brenda. I don't think you did any damage.

Tom: That little ring is probably floating around at the top of the engine somewhere. It's unlikely to get in the way of any moving parts and break anything, although it may position itself in the way of an oil drain hole and keep some of the oil from draining properly.

Ray: That's not really a big deal, either. The real danger is if the plastic ring melts and plugs up something permanently. I don't know the melting point of that particular type of plastic, but it's probably higher than your typical oil temperature, which is around 300 degrees Fahrenheit. And my guess is that if it was going to melt, it would have done so already, and you'd be writing to us asking about the price of Saturn's replacement engines.

Tom: So, if it were my car, I'd leave it alone. Then, next time you need a new valve-cover gasket, ask your mechanic if he can fish out the ring, which is certain to be sitting someplace on top of the cylinder head. If he asks why you want a plastic ring, tell him it was your grandmother's and it's of great sentimental value to you.

THE BODY IN THE BACK OF THE VAN

Dear Tom and Ray:

I recently purchased a used Dodge Caravan SE. I really enjoy it but am wondering about a thudding noise that sounds a little like a dead body rolling around in the back of the van every time I accelerate quickly. I asked my neighbor about it, and he says his Caravan makes the exact same noise. He thinks it's a design glitch. The spare tire seems secure, and neither one of us works for the Mafia. What's up?

—Barb

Tom: A word of advice, Barb. Leave the Mafia jokes to us. We're already in the Witness Protection Program.

Ray: You mean the "witless" protection program.

Tom: The most likely cause of your noise is a loose piece of the exhaust pipe hitting the floor, the right rear shock absorber, the leaf spring, or something else in the back. When you accelerate, you change the angle of the chassis relative to the ground, and that could cause a loose or improperly installed exhaust pipe to hit something and make a "buh-bum" noise.

Ray: Of course it's also possible that the noise is due to Chrysler's top-secret Caravan Recycling Automation Program, often referred to by its acronym.

Tom: Our theory is that as part of this innovative program, immediately after delivery, the vehicle's parts begin to loosen up by themselves as you drive around. And while many owners think these are design flaws or mechanical problems, we believe they're actually part of a carefully thought-out plan to make the Caravan easier to recycle at the end of its life.

Ray: But if you don't buy that, have your mechanic check the exhaust system, Barb. You'll probably find the source of the noise there.

NO RADIO IN REVERSE

Dear Tom and Ray:

This one has stumped a number of car shops, and it has a funny element to it. About a month ago, my wife was backing our 1997 Mercury Sable out of the drive-way. As soon as she put it in reverse, the radio cut off. As soon as the automatic transmission was shifted into any other gear, the radio came back on. My first reaction was: "This is a new safety device. Somehow, the car figured out how to tell when my wife is behind the wheel and, given her general difficulties driving a car in reverse, wanted to eliminate all possible distractions." Unfortunately, the car isn't that smart, and it does it when either of us is driving. Do you experts have any idea what would cause this?

—Ted

Ray: Well, I'm going to guess that it's very cold and damp in your garage, Ted. And if I were you, I'd start by installing some sort of heating system.

Tom: You think the cold and dampness in his garage is causing his radio to cut out?

Ray: No. But after his wife sees that nasty comment he made, he's going to be sleeping there, so he might as well make it comfortable.

Tom: Truthfully, Ted, this is not a problem we can solve for you without checking under the hood; it's a problem that a mechanic has to investigate in person. There's no direct connection between the back-up lights, for instance, and the radio. But we can give you a few suggestions about where to look.

Ray: One item to check is the ignition switch. Sometimes, if an ignition switch is worn out and isn't staying exactly in the "run" position, you can lose accessories. Why it would happen only in reverse, I don't know, but the shift lever is in that same general area. So when the car is in reverse and the radio cuts out, try gently moving the ignition key around and see if you can get the radio to come back. If you can, my money is on the switch.

Tom: Another consideration is that the whole engine shifts when you put the car in gear. It moves in one direction when you put the car in drive, and in exactly the opposite direction when you put it in reverse. It's possible that when you shift into reverse and the engine moves, it might tug on a ground wire or stretch a connection somewhere. This condition would be made worse if you have a worn motor mount (the large rubber insulators that are supposed to hold the engine in place). And we replace lots of motor mounts on these cars.

Ray: It could also be a loose wiring harness at the fire wall, or any number of things that we can't identify for you; but with the car in front of him, a mechanic ought to be able to figure this out pretty easily. He'll check the ignition switch and start jiggling wires until he makes the radio cut out, and then he'll know exactly where the problem is.

Tom: Meanwhile, don't forget to make sure your garage door is shut all the way before you go to sleep, Ted. It not only gets drafty, but when the raccoons climb on top of you in the middle of the night it'll scare the hell out of you.

MY WIFE'S BUTT IS HOT

Dear Tom and Ray:

My wife's butt is so hot—and it was caused by our 2003 Ford Focus wagon's seat warmers! The seat warmers burned the seat material and my wife's new winter coat! I wrote Ford's consumer affairs department to warn them of a very serious burn/fire hazard. All I got back was some goofy letter about being unable to offer any assistance with our claim. We didn't submit a claim! We just wanted Ford to look into this safety issue so that nobody gets hurt! We filed a report with the NTSB. Anyplace else we should contact regarding this?

—Bill

Ray: Well, we're glad you spoke to the NTSB—the National Association of Toasted and Singed Butts.

Tom: Actually, NTSB—the National Transportation Safety Board—is the wrong place for this. It investigates airplane crashes and stuff like that. And while it may have seemed nearly that dire when your wife was doing the lambada in the seat, the place to go is NHTSA, the National Highway Traffic Safety Administration. They're the people who handle auto safety.

Ray: You should definitely report this to NHTSA. You can do it from the organization's Web site, www.safercar.gov, or through the auto-safety hotline, 1-888-327-4236.

Tom: And, in fact, we checked the list of customer safety complaints (which you can do, too), and there have already been a few reports of overheating seat warmers on Ford Focuses. So I'm sure NHTSA will be interested in hearing from you. If they get enough complaints about a certain safety problem, they can open an investigation, which can eventually lead to a safety recall.

Ray: But in the meantime, you should get this fixed! I mean, it might be a fun trick to play on your passengers, but you don't want to create any actual griddle marks on anybody's tuchus. Or start a fire.

Tom: So take the car to your dealer and ask him to investigate. There should be a resistor that limits the amount of current the heating element is allowed to pull. That resistor, or the element itself, may be faulty.

Ray: And on your way home from the dealership, be a nice guy and pick up a gift for your wife. See what's on sale at Victoria's Flame-Retardant Secret.

I HAVE A FIVE-SPEED PROPECIA-MOBILE!

Dear Tom and Ray:

This morning I went to my car to find it had grown what appeared to be hair from the tailpipe. It was about 10 inches long and gray with brown highlights. I had to get to class, so I gave my car a haircut with my Swiss Army knife. I tried to pull the rest out of the tailpipe, but it wouldn't budge. I am continuing to drive my car. What came out of the back end of my car? Should I get it checked? Any advice on how to tell a mechanic about this without sounding like I've lost my mind?

—Samantha

Ray: Well, Samantha, the first thing I'd do is contact Sy Sperling at the Hair Club for Men to see about becoming a supplier. If this continues, you could pay off your student loans, and then some.

Tom: We've actually seen this before, Samantha. It's muffler hair. Some cars (we've seen it on Hondas) use a fibrous insulating material as a sound-deadener in their mufflers. When the muffler starts to deteriorate, the stuff starts to come off, and it heads out through the tailpipe. And you're right—it looks and feels just like hair. I find it quite disgusting and creepy, actually.

Ray: What it's made of, I don't know. But now that you mention it, I have seen a large fleet of Accords in the Hair Club for Men parking lot.

Tom: So, what to do? In the short run, I'd apply some leave-in conditioner. That'll make it more manageable.

Ray: Actually, you can keep driving the car, but this means that your muffler is on the way out. And sooner rather than later, the car is going to get real loud. So if you've got the money, you might as well replace the muffler now, Samantha.

MY LEXUS IS MISSING ITS CUSH

Dear Tom and Ray:

I have a six-year-old Lexus ES with 68,000 miles on it. Great car. No problems except that my driver's seat has lost its "cush." My tush is sore and uncomfortable after a long drive. This didn't happen when it was new. What can a tender tush do? Replace the seat? Put another cushion on top (which would take away valuable headroom)? Replace the padding inside the seat (a difficult and messy job)? Or get a chauffeur? I suspect this is a common problem for aging cars. I don't want to unload the best car I have ever had just because I am unhappy with the seat.

—Will

Ray: The problem may not be the car's seat, Will. It's been six years since you bought this car, and you may be suffering from P.T.E. (Progressive Tush Enlargement).

Tom: It happens to people our age, Will. Look at my brother. He's got what the airlines call a two-ticket butt.

Ray: In your case, Will, you have a lot of options. You've got an otherwise great car, which you love. You've only got 68,000 miles on it, and you can probably expect at least another 68,000 out of it. So the answer, in your case, is to replace the seat.

Tom: Right. On a heap like my '63 Dodge Dart, you'd toss a boat cushion on top, or just wrap it in a bunch of duct tape. But on a well-preserved Lexus, you fix the seat.

Ray: And you can either ask your dealer to order a new set of cushions for you from Lexus and install them (without the leather covers, the cushions run about $250), or you can get a good upholstery shop to make a new cushion for you. That'll be cheaper. And they may even be able to customize it to fit your shape.

Tom: Just insist they leave room for future expansion, Will.

"CLEAN ME!"

Dear Tom and Ray:

Does writing in the dirt/dust on a car scratch the paint? A teacher at my children's school today wrote "Clean Me" as a joke in the dirt on my new Suburban as I was parked in the school pickup line. (It was dirty only because we've had bad weather lately!) I had left it unattended while I was visiting another mother ahead of me in line, waiting for the kids to come out of school. I'm a little surprised that an adult male would do this, and I don't quite know how to bring up the subject with him. I don't want to hurt his feelings, but I do want him to know that I didn't appreciate the fact that he could have scratched the paint. I haven't had a new vehicle since 1999, and it really hurt my feelings to have someone do this the second week I've owned the vehicle. How can I give this fella an education about not messing with other people's cars without offending him?

—Linda

Ray: Well, first of all, Linda, you should never be surprised at what an adult male will do. In the big scheme of adult-male misdeeds, however, this is not something for the International Court of Justice in The Hague.

Tom: I know what I'd do. I'd write "Clean Me" on *his* car. With a nail!

Ray: You see what I mean about adult males, Linda? If there was nothing but dust or fine particles of dirt on the car, it's unlikely to have done any damage. However, if there was grit and sand on the car, it's possible that there are some slight scratches on your paint. In that case, rest assured that the scratches will easily come out with some polishing compound.

Tom: As you know, cars get scratches all the time. The back of someone's jacket rubs against your door in a parking lot; someone puts a shopping bag on the hood; your kid rubs her backpack against it while getting in; you scrape up against a bush in a driveway. Scratches are inevitable, and there's no avoiding them over time. So don't lose sleep over it.

Ray: On the other hand, you can say to the fellow: "Listen, I know you were just joking around, but you probably didn't know that you can scratch the car that way. And since it's a brand-new car, I'm not emotionally ready to have it scratched up yet!"

Tom: "And, by the way, you owe me $5,000 for a paint job!"

Ray: See? Adult males. Be nice about it, Linda, because I'm sure the guy didn't think he was doing any harm. But letting him know will make you feel better and will force him to find alternative ways to be destructive in the future.

SACRED MALE

BONDING RITUALS

The Truth About Guys and Cars

SACRED MALE BONDING RITUALS

Dear Tom and Ray:

Being as you are males of the species and you know a heck of a lot about cars, perhaps you can explain why menfolk tend to give their cars a burst of gas as they turn them off. Should I do that, or is it some sacred macho bonding ritual? Love your column!

—Nancie

Ray: You've hit the nail right on the head, Nancie. It's a sacred male bonding ritual with no mechanical value whatsoever.

Tom: In the early days of civilization, some fathers taught their sons that it was important to give the car a little gas as you turned it off. The theory was that this would fill up the carburetor bowl with gasoline and make the engine easier to start next time.

Ray: This theory was dubious back then. And since (A) all carburetors manufactured since the Eisenhower administration come with accelerator pumps to get the car started and (B) all modern cars are fuel injected and don't even have carburetors, the theory is now under intense scrutiny by the S.A.E., the A.P.I., the N.O.W., and even the NAACP (National Association for the Advancement of Carbureted Products).

Tom: But if the menfolk in your clan want to perform this sacred bonding ritual, Nancie, I'd say, let them. After all, it's a lot less messy than, say, animal sacrifice.

FRAGILE EGOS

Dear Tom and Ray:

You guys are always putting down men when it comes to automotive knowledge. You almost always publish incidents where the woman is right and the hubby—or some other guy—is wrong. Are you guys afraid of women?

—Rudy

Tom: No. We just believe it's important to state publicly that men don't always know what they're talking about just because the subject is cars.

Ray: And we think it is incumbent upon us to tell the American public that in our experience fixing cars, women are better at describing problems, better at answering questions about symptoms, and, in general, have less of their ego tied up in pretending that they know everything.

Tom: Why do we feel the need to make these things clear in writing so frequently, Rudy?

Ray: Well, because our wives told us to.

THE TRUTH ABOUT GUYS AND CARS

Dear Tom and Ray:

My husband and I really enjoy your column. I have a story for you about brothers and cars. My husband's brother John has two older cars. The transmission went on his favorite beater, so he had to do some "minor" repairs on the other heap to get it running again. It's a 1982 Buick LeSabre, and it needed headlights and a starter. John has very little knowledge of engines but proceeds to start dismantling parts to extract the starter. After a few hours of not really knowing what he's doing, he calls Roger (my husband) and asks for help. My husband is not a mechanic, but he's done some repairs and has basic common sense. So he helps John get the starter out and goes with him to buy a replacement, and together they put it back in. John (with no sense) telling Roger (common sense) how to do it. Roger likes his little brother, so he listens and does as John says, crossed wires, misaligned screws, and all. Of course, the car won't start. Roger comes home and tells me the story, and I ask him why he listened to John if he knew John was wrong. He shrugs. Next day, Roger goes back and reconnects the starter as it should be and the car starts. But why didn't he do that in the first place? Is brotherly love that deep, or is this a "man thing"? Please clue me in.

—Dawn

Tom: I can totally sympathize, Dawn. I like my little brother, Ray, but he's wrong most of the time, too. I don't know why I keep listening to him.

Ray: The reason you listen to me is that even though I'm wrong most of the time, I'm right more often than you are, because you're wrong all the time.

Tom: The truth is, men communicate better when they're grunting and groaning. Most men think—deep down inside—that sharing their feelings makes them sissies. And they don't want to be sissies. So they figure if they're torquing head bolts and repacking wheel bearings, who could possibly question their manhood? So under the hood, they feel free to share their true feelings about things. In fact, if you listen carefully under the hood of a car, you can usually hear two men talking about fear, vulnerability, acceptance, and pure love.

Ray: And there's historical precedent for this. In the old days, cavemen would discuss these things when they were clubbing a wooly mammoth or moving a big rock.

Tom: So, you see, this is an ancient communication ritual, Dawn, and it would be a bad idea to interrupt it. If the two brothers don't have this precious time together under the hood—and letting John screw up is just Roger's way of extending that time—they may never be able to speak to each other.

Ray: Or worse—they may start looking for things to fix around *your* house.

A JERK IN MY OLDSMOBILE

Dear Tom and Ray:

I have an '88 Olds Cutlass Ciera. A few months ago, my wife was in the process of slowing down to stop on an exit ramp. The vehicle started jerking as though the engine would die. By the time she came to a complete stop, the engine had, in fact, died. Using the ignition, she immediately restarted the engine. There was no more occurrence of this experience for the next several weeks until we took a long trip of about five hours. When we pulled off the highway to stop in a small town, the vehicle bucked and stalled again. It has not done it for the last four weeks. Could this be happening because the engine has stopped firing instead of going into the idle mode?

—Phil

Tom: You've just illustrated beautifully a major difference between men and women when it comes to cars, Phil. If your wife had come to us, she would have said something like, "The car stalls sometimes when I stop after a long drive."

Ray: To which we would have asked a few questions and said, "Okay, we'll take a look at it."

Tom: Whereas you, Phil, said, "Could this be happening because the engine has stopped firing instead of going into the idle mode?"

Ray: To which most mechanics would say, "Absolutely, Phil, probably due to a misaligned anti-bozerus valve and an overextended multiplatinum port socket. Big money, Phil. But an excellent diagnosis!"

Tom: And you would have forked over $1,200 and walked away proud that you sounded like you knew what you were talking about.

Ray: For some reason, men feel a need to act as if they know what's wrong. Whereas we believe you get better service from a mechanic if you tell him the symptoms and let him make the diagnosis. That way you won't inadvertently lead him astray (remember, most of us mechanics aren't that bright and are easily swayed) and, more important, he's then responsible if the thing he replaces doesn't fix the problem.

Tom: Anyway, if I had to guess, I'd say your problem is a faulty lock-up torque converter in your automatic transmission. The lock-up converter locks the car into gear at higher speeds—as if it were a manual transmission—to eliminate slippage and save gasoline. Every so often, yours isn't unlocking. And if you've ever driven a manual transmission and come to a stop while forgetting to put your foot on the clutch, you know what happens; the car bucks and stalls. And that's exactly what's happening to your little Ciera.

Ray: A dealer or transmission shop can perform one of two repairs for you. They can simply unplug the lock-up converter and you can do without it (and the increased mileage that it brings). Or you can have it fixed for a few hundred dollars. And if you're planning on keeping the car for a while, I'd recommend fixing it. But let your wife take the car in for you, Phil.

A HEATED ARGUMENT

Dear Tom and Ray:

I live in Portland, Maine (cold winters), and I own a brand-new Nissan Pathfinder. My husband told me that on winter mornings I should leave the temperature knob all the way to the "cold" position until my engine heats up. He says this will allow my engine to warm up properly and will be better for my engine. I want to leave the temperature knob all the way on "hot" with the fan off. Then once I start feeling some heat seeping in, I'll turn on the fan. He tells me that this will reduce the life of my engine and that if I keep doing it I'll start experiencing problems. Is he right?

—Carrie

Ray: This is the kind of thing that men spend hours and hours contemplating, Carrie.

Tom: Hours? Years! I mean, there's probably not a man alive who hasn't wondered about the proper position of the heat knob while the car is warming up.

Ray: And because your husband has given so much thought to this, it would be a severe blow to his ego if you were to prove him wrong, Carrie. He might never recover from it.

Tom: So we're not going to print here that it makes no difference what you do with the temperature knob.

Ray: Right. We'll explain that to you in a private little note we're going to send later.

Tom: Let's just say, in print, for the record, that your husband is technically correct. Because the heat exchanger under the dashboard is just like another radiator, it does take some heat away from the engine. So leaving the temperature knob in the "hot" position will cause the engine to take a little longer to warm up. How much longer? A few seconds? A minute? I don't know.

Ray: But as we'll explain in our private letter to you later, Carrie, it's so insignificant that it won't make any meaningful difference in the life or reliability of the engine. So for practical purposes, you can do whatever you want and not worry about it.

Tom: Moreover, what's more important? The life of the engine or the temperature of your fingers? Let's get serious here. Right, Carrie?

Ray: So now you face the classic marital dilemma: Would you rather be right, or would you rather be happy?

Tom: Well, believe it or not, we have a solution that allows you to be both. Invest in a block heater. For people who live in the great frozen tundra like you guys, an electric block heater is a wonderful thing. You plug it in to a timer so it heats up your coolant a couple hours before you start the car in the morning. And then you have instant heat and instant engine operating temperature.

Ray: That keeps your fingers warm, your engine warm, and the home fires burning, if you know what I mean. Sounds like the perfect anniversary gift to me. In fact, isn't the tenth anniversary the block-heater anniversary?

MALE ANSWER SYNDROME STRIKES AGAIN

Dear Tom and Ray:

About a month ago we bought a new Ford from a local dealer. It was a demonstrator model and had about 6,000 miles on it. The dealer agreed to do some minor repairs that we requested, and he said if we noticed anything else in the next few weeks we should bring it to his attention. After about two weeks of driving I saw that moisture kept forming on the inside of the right front headlight. My husband talked to the salesman about it, and the salesman said that because it is a halogen bulb, the headlight can't be sealed too tightly. He said that otherwise it would heat up so much that the inside of the headlight would melt. When my husband related this story to me, I asked, "Well, does that mean the other headlight is going to melt, since it's obviously sealed tightly enough to keep out water? And shouldn't other people's headlights be melting, since I don't see moisture forming in their headlights?" Could you please explain what's going on?

—Susie

Ray: I guess you didn't hear the end of the dealer's sentence, Susie. He said, "If you notice anything in the next few weeks, bring it to our attention. And *then* we'll tell you to get lost."

Tom: The salesman either was lying to you, or he's afflicted with Male Answer Syndrome—the need by many men to provide an authoritative-sounding answer despite the fact that they have no idea what they're talking about. My brother and I both have it (as you shall see below).

Ray: This might have been exacerbated by Commissioned Salesperson Syndrome—the willingness of a salesperson to do or say anything to make a sale—and conversely, to do or say anything to get rid of anyone not actively involved in buying something.

Tom: The salesman has got his headlight in his taillight socket, Susie. The entire headlight fixture is sealed tight at the factory. Why is it sealed? So moisture won't get in and shorten the life of the bulb!

Ray: My guess is that you need a new headlight lens. What happens sometimes is that the headlight lens gets cracked. The cracks are usually very small and difficult to see. They usually come from pebbles and other debris that come up off the road. You often see this in older cars that have been pounded by road debris for years, but it can happen to a car of any age.

Tom: When you drive at 60 mph in the rain, water gets forced through those invisible cracks and it forms a film of moisture on the inside of the lens. Once it's in there, it can't escape, because there's no equivalent force pushing it out from the inside.

Ray: So here's what you do, Susie. Drive backward at 60 mph.

Tom: No. Go back to the dealer and ask him to replace the headlight fixture on the right side. Insist on it. He owes it to you.

CUTLASS BABE MAGNET

Dear Tom and Ray:

My 1994 Olds Cutlass Ciera has been a great car for 50,000 miles. I'm wondering if it could be made to handle better. It's a little bouncy, and it sways a little when it corners. Do you think if I got the right combination of new tires and shocks it would corner like a Corvette? And if it starts handling like a Corvette, will women suddenly become more interested in me? Or do I need to start smoking a pipe and wearing a smoking jacket and ascot for that?

—AJ

Ray: My brother used to wear an ascot. But then he got his ascot caught in the fan one day, and that was the end of that.

Tom: You can't make this handle like a Corvette, AJ! C'mon! This car doesn't have a very sophisticated suspension to begin with. It doesn't have four-wheel independent suspension, nor does it have a particularly stiff chassis. So no matter what you do to it, no one's ever going to mistake it for a sports car.

Ray: However, new tires and working shocks will make a big difference if you need them. So that's the place to invest some money if you feel it used to handle better than it does now. But get someone to check the shocks and tires for you first.

Tom: One other important thing about the Corvette, AJ. We've discovered through meticulous research that Corvettes (and cars like them), contrary to popular male belief, do not attract the attention of women. They tend to attract the attention of men, who *think* they attract the attention of women. Women tend to be frightened or intimidated by them.

Ray: Don't get me wrong. This Cutlass Ciera of yours is no babe magnet. But if you're really interested in attracting the attention of women, forget the Corvette and try getting something cute, like a Miata, a RAV4, or, better yet, a puppy!

THE KARMANN GHIA OF
HEARTBREAK

Cars and Relationships

THE KARMANN GHIA OF HEARTBREAK

Dear Tom and Ray:

Around 1962, I had a girlfriend who had a new VW Karmann Ghia roadster. We were students at UC Berkeley. This is hilly country, and when she parked the car on a relatively level area it would start. If she parked on a slope, it was completely dead. If it was pushed from the slope to a level area it would fire right up. Yes, she tried the dealer, but to no avail. I was a hot-rod owner and knew a little, and I tried everything I could think of. I never solved the problem, and she left me. What was the solution?

—Gordon

Ray: Well, we can't be sure, Gordon, but I'm guessing you lost the love of your life over a 99-cent part.

Tom: Lots of these old Volkswagens suffered from bad starter bushings. There was a bushing—about the size of the tip of your little finger—that supported the end of the starter-motor shaft. The bushing was housed inside the engine block. If that bushing was bad and allowed the starter shaft to get even a little bit out of alignment, the car would refuse to crank.

Ray: We used to find these bad bushings when people would complain that their Karmann Ghias would intermittently fail to start—*and* after we unsuccessfully put three or four new starters in their cars. I never connected it specifically to hills, but it certainly is possible that the angle of the car could have caused the geometry of the starter to shift and caused this problem.

Tom: And to fix it, you needed to extract the bad bushing and replace it. If it's any comfort to you, Gordon, it probably wasn't a job you would have been able to do yourself. It was a pain in the butt and required a couple of special tools. So don't feel bad.

Ray: By the way, we also heard from your old girlfriend recently. She was having her '62 Karmann Ghia restored—with the money she won in the megabucks lottery. She wanted to give her husband something to drive when he didn't feel like driving the Ferrari or cabin cruiser she bought him.

THE REAR REASON FOR SPOILERS

Dear Tom and Ray:

It's my understanding that spoilers are used to increase high-speed traction on the drive wheels of a car. That being the case, what is the purpose of a spoiler on the rear of a front-wheel-drive car?

—Barry

Ray: The main purpose of spoilers is getting dates, Barry. Of course, it's never worked for me, even though I've had a spoiler on the back of my '87 Dodge Dakota pickup truck for years.

Tom: Theoretically, spoilers do serve a marginally useful purpose. They're designed to use the wind—when the car is traveling at high speed—to force the rear end of the car downward. That's supposed to help keep the rear wheels planted more firmly on the pavement, which helps you maintain traction.

Ray: And the reason that's useful, even with front wheel drive, is that no matter which wheels are powered by the engine, it's still a good idea to have all four wheels on the ground, Jim Rockford notwithstanding. Even if you're driving a front-wheel-drive car, you want those rear wheels firmly on the ground for cornering, braking, and just plain stability.

Tom: But the truth is, at 55 or 65 miles an hour, spoilers don't do much. They're designed for race cars that take corners at 120 miles an hour—speeds at which wheels can actually start to lift off the ground. And in those situations, they can really make a difference. But in day-to-day driving, they serve the same societal purpose as tattoos and hair replacements.

IN SEARCH OF A LITTLE CLASS

Dear Tom and Ray:

I have an eleven-year-old Acura Integra with 85,000 miles. For the greater part of seven years, the fan/blower has worked fine. Recently, it started not coming on right away. It takes from two to ten minutes for it to start up in either heat or AC mode. My girlfriend has threatened to leave me for someone with more class if this problem is not resolved quickly. What should I do?

—Ralph

Tom: This is an easy one, Ralph. I'd dump her.

Ray: Me, too. If that's all it takes for her to threaten to leave, I don't think she's going to be a very reliable mate. I'd break it off now.

Tom: After that, you might want to replace the fan relay. That should take care of that other little problem you mentioned in your letter.

COVET NOT THY HARDBODY

Dear Tom and Ray:

My husband has a 1989 Nissan Hardbody truck (I don't know what a hard body is, but he likes talking about it). The truck has been great, with only one problem— the red paint oxidizes terribly. Therefore, my husband spends hours rubbing some kind of cream all over the truck to get it to shine beautifully so he can admire it. Then, after a couple of weeks, it oxidizes again. Any help you can give me so my husband can spend more time admiring me and less time on his truck would be greatly appreciated.

—Susan

Tom: Wow, Susan! My fingers are still burning from reading your letter!

Ray: We felt like the nuances of this were too hot for us to handle, Susan. So we faxed a copy of your question over to America's foremost sex therapist, Dr. Ruth Westheimer. And Dr. Ruth was kind enough to give us her suggestion. (Really! We're not kidding.)

Dr. Ruth: *Dear Susan, I'm not an expert on the bodies of cars. I had to giggle at your question. I have a suggestion. Take another car—not the car in question with which your husband is having a "love affair." Then, put a basket for a picnic hidden in the trunk. Include champagne. If it's evening, bring some candlelight and some mosquito repellant, and drive to a secluded place. Have a blanket in the car, and provide him with the best sexual experience he has ever had. I leave the position up to you. Let me know if it works. Sincerely, Dr. Ruth*

Tom: Wow. It really pays to go to an expert. We never would have come up with an answer like that!

Ray: Yeah. We were going to suggest something boring like taking the truck to an autobody shop to have it compounded.

Tom: Compound is a mild abrasive that actually removes the oxidized outer layer of paint and gives you a new surface from which to start. If the oxidation is too deep and compounding doesn't help, and he's still interested in the truck after your picnic, you'll have to get it repainted.

Ray: But pick a color other than red next time. Red paint, as you know all too well, Susan, requires a lot of attention to keep it looking good.

BEING POSITIVE ABOUT POSITRACTION

Dear Tom and Ray:

I called two Chevy dealers and one four-wheel-drive specialist and got three differ-ent answers. Then I talked with my boyfriend, who happens to be very mechanically inclined, and that was the icing on the cake of confusion. I own a Chevy full-size pickup with four-wheel drive, and I need to know whether positraction is different from limited slip differential. I also need to know what I have on my truck. I got stuck in three-and-a-half feet of snow! I have a bet with my boyfriend riding on the answer, so I hope you can clear it up.

—Jeannie

Ray: You want us to clear this up, Jeannie??? This happens to be one of the most perplexing questions of the late 20th century. Chevrolet alone has four full-time philosophers and a periodontist working on this issue as we speak.

Tom: Actually, Jeannie, "positraction" is just Chevrolet's name for limited slip dif-ferential on passenger cars.

Ray: Normally, on a rear-wheel-drive car, the power is delivered to both rear wheels equally. But because of the way the differential works, when one wheel starts to slip, all the power is then delivered to *that* wheel. That doesn't help you much if that wheel is stuck on snow or ice.

Tom: To correct for that design problem, limited slip differential automatically transfers some of the power from the slipping wheel to the other wheel. That's why it helps you get off a patch of ice or snow.

Ray: On Chevy trucks, limited slip is called a "locking differential." That's just a heavier-duty version of positraction, and it operates *only* on the rear wheels, even if you have four-wheel drive.

Tom: So what do you have on your truck, Jeannie? Well, we don't know. We know you don't have positraction, because that's only available on cars. You may have a locking differential, but you haven't given us enough information to know that. The fact that you got stuck in three-and-a-half feet of snow doesn't tell us anything. You're *supposed* to get stuck in three-and-a-half feet of snow, even if you have eight-wheel drive.

Ray: So there are several other ways to find out how your truck is equipped. The easiest way is to check your original dealer invoice. If you've lost that, which we assume you have, you can check the equipment decal, which is pasted to the bottom of the glove box. If you see the code "G80" on the equipment decal, that tells you the truck has a locking differential.

Tom: Or, if you want to do some real-world experimentation, we suggest the Felipo Berrio test. Put the truck in your garage and put it in two-wheel drive. Then pour a quart of Felipo Berrio extra-virgin olive oil (make sure it's extra-virgin) under the right rear wheel.

Ray: Next, have your boyfriend step on the gas. If the wheel just spins, you don't have a locking differential. If, on the other hand, the truck shoots forward into the bicycles, the storm windows, and the old tires, then you do have a locking differential. Congratulations!

HE LOOKS SO CUTE WHEN HE'S BALANCING A TIRE

Dear Tom and Ray:

I need some help. You see, I have a crush on my mechanic, but I can't seem to bring myself to just ask him on a date or ask if he has a significant other. I keep stopping in with questions about my truck, but I'm running out of those, as well as money to have things fixed. I'm not picking up any vibes from him. Do you have any suggestions?

—**No Names Please**

Tom: Well, if he hasn't noticed you yet, he's unlike any living mechanic we've ever met, NNP.

Ray: Here's what I would do. I'd get a yellow legal pad and I'd start to compose a personals ad. Include your age, a modest description of yourself (young, vivacious, etc.) and some of your interests. Then include a line that says something like, "Loves guys who can fix things."

Tom: Then conveniently leave this work-in-progress on the passenger seat of your truck with the pen sitting on top of it.

Ray: Then go in and tell Mr. Hotwrench that you're hearing a strange noise in the passenger compartment. Tell him it's intermittent and that it occurs every five minutes or so, so he'll have to sit in the truck with the engine running for five minutes until he hears it.

Tom: That should do it. He'll be sitting in your truck, bored, with nothing to do. He'll inevitably look around and see the personals ad you're working on. And if he has any interest whatsoever, that should give him all the encouragement he needs.

Ray: And if you really want to seal the deal, add to your personal ad, "Loves to drink beer, watch sports on TV, and have the guys over for poker." And then throw a Victoria's Secret catalog on the dashboard.

IS HE WHAT HE DRIVES?

Dear Tom and Ray:

I have become very interested in someone and I'm trying to decide if I should ask him out or not. I noticed that he drives a Subaru Forester, and I cannot figure out what that says about the kind of guy he is. Possibly adventurous? Reliable? Any insight into this would be greatly appreciated. Thanks.

—Melissa

Tom: What a great question, Melissa! We all know that a person's car is like a 3,000-pound rolling personality test, so why not analyze the car before getting involved? I mean, I used to drive a 1952 MG TD. What more do you need to know about me? I'm fun, I'm loyal, and I'm a classic!

Ray: Not to mention dilapidated, hopelessly out of date, and hard to start in the morning! Now, in my case, I drive a 1997 Honda Odyssey. So you know that I'm just what you need, and nothing extravagant. I'm practical, reliable, and not overly showy.

Tom: Not to mention peeling on top, wide in the back end, and of questionable exhaust habits.

Ray: Well, as you can see, Melissa, descriptions like these can cut both ways. So we'll give you both sides of your Subaru Forester guy.

Tom: First, let's go straight from Subaru's marketing material: "Engineered to deliver safety, comfort, and high performance, the Forester achieves excellence on all levels. And with its good looks and exceptional value, Forester is the ideal choice for the discerning driver."

Ray: But if you read between the lines, you could interpret those same words as meaning that he's too careful, comfortable but not exciting, and "performs" at a high level but is rarely at that high level naturally. If someone has to protest that he looks good—well, you can figure out what that means, Melissa. Finally, "value" suggests he's a cheapskate.

Tom: I hope we've helped, Melissa. Please do write back and let us know how it turns out. America is dying to know!

PSYCHOANALYZING A MIDLIFE-CRISIS POWER CURVE

Dear Tom and Ray:

I hope you can help settle an issue between me and my psychoanalyst husband. It's about how to drive my Saturn SL2. My hubby went out and bought a BMW motorcycle this past spring. Since then he's announced that we've been driving the Saturn wrong for the past ten years. He thinks we should wait until the engine reaches at least 4,000 rpm to shift into the next higher gear. ("The red zone isn't until 6,500 rpm!") He supports this assertion with talk of driving with the power curve so that he can have optimal acceleration or something like that. When I point out that the panel shows the orange arrow suggesting that he shift up at about 2,000 rpm, he calls it an "idiot light." I want this engine to last at least another five years. I'm afraid, though, that he might kill the engine or transmission. Or, from the way the engine sounds when he drives, that he might take off and fly into space—and since we live near Washington, D.C., he might be shot down as a potential terrorist. Help!

—Sallie

Ray: Well, if you really want this engine to last another five years, you need to go to the Saturn dealer and have him change the ignition key. And then don't give your husband a copy of the new one.

Tom: Yeah. I'm kind of surprised that, as a psychoanalyst, he doesn't recognize that he's going through some sort of midlife crisis. I mean, the BMW motorcycle, the power curves—it can't get much more obvious, Sallie. I'd keep my eye out for hidden copies of *Naked Coed Adventure Travel* magazine if I were you.

Ray: Here's the problem. Your husband is not wrong. He's just nuts. You two clearly want different things out of your vehicles. He wants to get as much power as possible out of the engine (ask the analyst why he feels he's lacking in power, Sallie). And if he wants maximum power out of his engine, he's right to shift near the top of the power curve, which is probably around 4,000 rpm in this car.

Tom: But if you want the best fuel economy, the greatest longevity from an engine, or the fewest dirty looks from friends, neighbors, and other drivers, you drive it gently and shift much earlier, like you do, Sallie.

Ray: So until this crisis of his passes, let him take out his power-curve aggressions on his motorcycle (provided you have good life insurance for him). But when the two of you take your car, you drive, and let him sit in the passenger seat and go "vroom, vroom."

SHIFTY BOYFRIEND

Dear Tom and Ray:

I have a 1993 Toyota Camry four-cylinder with an automatic transmission and overdrive. My girlfriend uses it occasionally and feels it's ridiculous to manually engage/disengage the overdrive when I tell her it's necessary to. Her point is, what's the use of having an automatic transmission if you have to shift it? She will soon be driving the car regularly, and I'm wondering if her leaving it in overdrive all the time will cause strain or worse problems for the transmission.

—Mike

Tom: Mike, pay attention, because we're going to ask you a very important question. Would you rather be right, or would you rather be happy?

Ray: Actually, it's not a terribly important question for you, Mike, since you're not going to be *either* this time. But it's a good question to keep in mind when future relational disputes arise.

Tom: In this case, your girlfriend is right. The automatic transmission shifts into the appropriate gear all by itself. Hence the name "automatic."

Ray: When the car gets going above a certain speed and you're not accelerating hard or climbing a hill, it shifts into overdrive to slow the engine and save gas.

Tom: And there's only one very specific condition under which you might want to take the transmission out of overdrive. If you're driving right at the speed where the transmission shifts from third gear to overdrive, you may find the transmission is "hunting."

Ray: That's the same thing baseball players do in the off-season. Only in this case it refers to the transmission shifting back and forth a lot looking for the right gear to be in.

Tom: And it doesn't hurt the transmission. It just has the capacity to be annoying to the driver. So if it bothers you, you can temporarily take the transmission out of overdrive until the road conditions change.

Ray: But if it doesn't bother you—and clearly, it doesn't bother your girlfriend as much as you're bothering her—you can just follow Bobby McFerrin's famous advice: Don't be shifty, be happy.

CAN'T GET GOOD HELP THESE DAYS

Dear Tom and Ray:

Recently my 1978 Dodge Aspen station wagon with almost 134,000 miles on it has developed a lot of annoying rattles around the back end and rear doors. At highway speed there is enough road noise to drown out the rattles, but the racket is distracting on city streets. My wife refuses to ride in back and help me pinpoint the rattles, and she refuses to drive the car so I can find the rattles myself. What do you suggest?

—*Bill*

Tom: Well, it sounds like a clear choice between a new wife and a new car, Bill. And frankly, since you've held tight to this piece of junk for over 130,000 miles, I'm a little worried about which way you're going to go.

Ray: This car was a heap in 1979, Bill. It's miraculous it's not on the scrap-metal boat to South Korea right now and somewhat terrifying for the rest of us that you still consider it roadworthy. It's time to face it. You may need new shocks, new springs, new spring shackles, new bushings between the body and the frame, or who knows what else. The car may be rusted out and ready to split in half!

Tom: These noises were designed into the car as a safety feature. So when the car starts to fall apart, these noises warn intelligent people to stay away from it. And that's why your wife won't drive it, Bill.

Ray: Get it to a mechanic and have him go over the whole car from top to bottom. It's dumb enough to endanger your marriage over a car. It's even dumber to endanger your life. But over a '78 Dodge Aspen wagon? C'mon, Bill! Get a life!

Massachusetts 08

CHPTR8

YOU MAY NEVER HAVE A CHANCE TO DO ANYTHING

THIS STUPID AGAIN!

In Defense of Impracticality and Following Your Heart

YOU MAY NEVER HAVE A CHANCE TO DO ANYTHING THIS STUPID AGAIN!

Dear Tom and Ray:

I'm getting ready to purchase my first automobile this summer and I have my heart set on an old British sports car. I'd like either an MG or a Triumph Spitfire. However, my parents aren't exactly thrilled because they feel old sports cars need too many repairs and are unsafe. I just want to drive to and from work, but I do want to know if cars like MGs and Spitfires are just a hassle.

—Kellie

Ray: A car like that is not just a hassle, Kellie, it's a complete and utter hassle as well as a money pit, a death trap, and source of continual and painful frustration.

Tom: But you should definitely get one, Kellie. They're wonderful cars!

Ray: In their favor, they are among the safest cars you can buy. They're always sitting in the driveway with the hood up, and you can't get much safer than that. And the buses you'll be taking instead do very well in crash tests.

Tom: Don't listen to him, Kellie, he has no sense of the romantic. He doesn't remember what it's like to cruise down the road, the roar of the engine in your ears, the sun on your face, and the wind tangling knots in your hair.

Ray: Very funny. I *do* remember what it's like to have hair for the wind to tangle. But when you painted this scene, you neglected to mention the smell of burning oil wafting up your nostrils and your AAA card clutched fearfully in your sweaty palm.

Tom: Oh, picky, picky. I've owned both these cars, and everything my brother says is true. But despite that, I have nothing but wonderful memories of them. Go for it, Kellie. Do it while you're young. You may never have another chance to do anything this stupid again!

MARGIE'S MIDLIFE CRISIS

Dear Tom and Ray:

I am having a genuine, bona fide midlife crisis. I can tell because I think I am acting the way all my friends say guys act when they have midlife crises. I want to ditch a perfectly good, reliable, almost-new Honda Accord and get a used, but not very old Volkswagen Vanagon. Not the camper, just the regular old Vanagon. Why? Because I'm sick of driving short cars in which everyone else's halogen lights shine directly into my eyes. Because I like sitting up straight instead of having my legs and lower back in stupid extended positions while driving. Because I'm tired of being sensible and buying sensible cars! I want something I can use for road trips, something up off the ground, something that will seat my friends and hold the plants I pick up when I stop suddenly at a nursery. I also want to be able to keep my clothes in it and sleep in it when I go to a weeklong camp and it rains! Am I crazy? I just paid off the Honda. And even if I am crazy, what vintage of Vanagon is most reliable? Help me either not do something stupid, or if I'm going to be stupid, help me do it in style, guys. Thanks.

—Margie

Tom: We'll help you do it in style, Margie!

Ray: I completely understand why you want to do this. In "perfecting" the automobile, Honda and Toyota have essentially turned cars into appliances. That's great for reliability. But do you ever get excited about your toaster oven? Does your Crock-Pot make you smile? Of course not. Your Honda is reliable and trustworthy, but it's boring.

Tom: And the Vanagon is just the opposite. Getting places will be an adventure in the Vanagon, Margie. Since you'll never know whether you're going to make it, you'll feel a thrill every time you do. And while driving down near the ground with lights in your eyes in the Honda is tedious, wait until you get blown around in a windstorm way up in that Vanagon. It's the next best thing to hang gliding!

Ray: I think this is a great move, Margie. After all, what is life if not an adventure? I'd go with the latest model Vanagon you can afford. I think Volkswagen made it up until about 1991. Then they redesigned it as a front-wheel-drive van and renamed it the Eurovan.

Tom: Either one will completely wipe out the memory of this boring Honda, Margie. But make sure your AAA membership is paid up before you pull the trigger, OK?

Dear Tom and Ray:

I am having a genuine, bona fide midlife crisis.

COROLLAS IN AFRICA

Dear Tom and Ray:

My daughter and I want to go to Africa, buy a car, and travel around for a year. I am fifty-three, she is twenty-two, and we are both in reasonably good health. We have agreed that if one of us begins to bleed from the eyeballs, the other one will shoot her (from a distance) and run. Neither of us is a good mechanic. What kind of vehicle would you buy, and where would you suggest buying it? I have thought about buying a Land Rover in England and then driving down to Africa. I would rather buy a used vehicle because of the cost, but we must have something very reliable. What do you two sages think? New or used? Where should we get it?

—Ann (for Ann and Shannon)

Ray: I'll tell you exactly what to do. You fly into Nairobi or wherever you're planning to start your trip. You make some local friends there, and you have them help you hire a guide/driver/translator/bodyguard for the year!

Tom: What you want is a guide who already owns a Toyota Land Cruiser (the official vehicle of sub-Saharan Africa). Most of them are old, but that tends to make them extremely fixable since they use nice, easy technologies like carburetors, points, and condensers. And any guide who owns one (and takes people out on trips) will be—by necessity—an experienced roadside mechanic, too.

Ray: And you make a deal with this guy to hire him and his Land Cruiser for the year. That way, you'll have an experienced driver, an onboard mechanic, a local translator, a cultural attaché, and someone to help you with whatever else comes up during your adventures—like hungry lions.

Tom: And, of course, someone who can shoot both of you if you both start bleeding through the eyeballs! Have a wonderful trip, you guys! And send us a postcard.

STIFF NECK

Dear Tom and Ray:

For years a friend of mine has been on me about something I did as a young man, which he says is harmful to any car. Many years ago, I drove my beat-up Chevy Vega (I know I am dating myself) to the Georgia bar exam, where the exam was administered. As I put the vehicle in reverse to park it, the clutch cable apparently broke. I had no clutch and the shifter was stuck in reverse. Being a penniless law-school student, after the exam that day (I was clearly exhausted mentally) I decided to drive the car home, going in reverse the entire ten-mile trip. It was difficult, looking backward over my shoulder, stopping at red lights on a busy street all the way home. Aside from the obvious traffic-law violations, my friend says it is BAD for any car to drive that far in reverse. I say it's not, since I got the cable repaired and drove the car for another two years. What do you say? Who is right?

—Steve

Ray: The good thing is you didn't do the car any harm. You might have harmed your career, if any future clients had seen you, but the car didn't suffer at all.

Tom: What you did is just like driving home in first gear. Your speed is limited because the gear ratio is high. But as long as you didn't go too fast and over-rev the engine, no harm was done.

Ray: And because of the difficulty of controlling a car while driving backward (as I'm sure you now know, Steve), I'm confident you *didn't* go too fast.

Tom: But by the way, Steve, you didn't have to drive home in reverse. When the clutch isn't working, you can still shift gears in a manual transmission if you first turn off the engine. So, you could have turned the engine off and shifted the car into, say, second gear, and driven home more comfortably—without getting a stiff neck. Remember that the next time this happens to your Vega, Steve!

HOW TO SEE AMERICA

Dear Tom and Ray:

In a few years I'm planning to take to the road in true hippie fashion and go "in search of America." I want to purchase a small, used camper-van for my wanderings. The obvious choice would seem to be a VW Microbus (or "V-Dub" in hippie parlance). I know there are plenty on the road right now that are older than their drivers. However, a friend of mine, experienced in such matters, recommends an American-made vehicle. His logic is that if you break down in, say, rural Texas, you could be several days trying to locate old VW parts, whereas most every small town in America has an old Ford or Dodge engine lying around. What do you guys recommend?

—Alan

Tom: Well, it may just be my age catching up with me, but if I were looking for America, Alan, I'd rent a Lincoln Town Car from Hertz. That way, if it breaks down in rural Texas, you can just leave it there and put a stick of dynamite in the tailpipe. Then call the 800 number and tell them that if they don't have a replacement vehicle there in two hours you're going to light it.

Ray: Actually, I agree with your friend. Not only are you more likely to be able to fix a Ford, Chevy, or Dodge van, but compared to the VW, it's likely to have all kinds of amenities you might find appealing, like decent handling, brakes, heat, and enough power to climb a hill or get out of its own way. As romantic an image as the VW Microbus has, the truth is that it was a dog of the first order, and unsafe to boot—with your legs protecting the rest of the vehicle in the event of a front-end collision.

Tom: Since you have so much time, Alan, I'd just buy a Ford, Chevy, or Dodge cargo van in good shape, and convert it yourself to a camper over the next few years. You can do the work yourself if you're mechanically inclined, or pay someone to do the work a little at a time as money becomes available.

Ray: I agree. You'd be much better off slapping a couple of McGovern bumper stickers on a Ford Econoline and dousing it with patchouli. Then you could have the whole hippie experience while still managing to get yourself across the Rocky Mountains.

I'M TELLIN' YA, THIS CAR IS BULLETPROOF!

Dear Tom and Ray:

For the past three years I've been living in the bush in Africa as an emergency relief coordinator. I generally travel in a Toyota Land Cruiser, and I have a couple of questions. First, if I get caught in an ambush, how fast can I go in reverse before blowing out the clutch? And second, the bullets from AK-47s go through a car door like paper. What can I do about that?

—*Bob*

Ray: First off, Bob, we want you to know that this is far beyond our capabilities. But then again, what isn't?

Tom: In terms of the bullets, I'd try complaining to OSHA. Aren't they supposed to deal with dangers in the workplace? I know they're busy dealing with repetitive stress syndrome from people using their computers too much, but maybe they could find time to look into this bullets-ripping-through-your-car-like-paper problem.

Ray: As for going in reverse, it won't hurt your clutch no matter how fast you go. But you could harm the engine. Reverse has a gear ratio about equal to first gear, which means by the time you're going 25 or 30 mph, the engine speed is going to be at or near the red line. So if you really stepped on it (which I imagine you would if you were running for your life), you could over-rev the engine and cause it to blow apart. And then you'd be facing that bullets-ripping-through-your-car-like-paper problem again.

Tom: You'd also discover that it's not easy to control a car when driving quickly in reverse. You're effectively steering with the rear wheels, and that creates some bizarre and difficult handling problems.

Ray: So what you want to do is get out of reverse as soon as possible. And to do that, you need to learn how to do a "Rockford." That's a skidding reversal of direction made famous—at least to us—by Jim Rockford on TV's *The Rockford Files*.

Tom: It's a stunt-driving trick that's easiest to do on some sort of slippery track. And dirt—which is probably what you're dealing with—would qualify.

Ray: It takes some dexterity and quite a bit of practice—especially in an SUV, which is easy to flip. But as you're traveling backward, you quickly cut the wheels all the way while pulling up on the parking brake. The back end of the car should stop and the front end should swing around past it. And as the front of the car is sliding past you, in one smooth maneuver you shift into drive or first gear, cut the wheel back the other way, release the hand brake, and pull out and keep going forward.

Tom: We should make clear that this is a stunt-driving maneuver and is not appropriate for the streets, so don't try this at home. You'll likely end up bashed into a curb with $5,000 worth of suspension damage, or rolled over and trying to explain to your wife what the hell you were doing.

Ray: But in your particular situation, Bob, it may be something you want to become familiar with. And if you get real good at it, let us know, and when you get back to the States, we'll see about getting you a job in pizza delivery.

DEAD BATTERY AS OPPORTUNITY

Dear Tom and Ray:

When should the battery be replaced in a car? My husband says that I should get a new one for my seven-year-old Olds Cutlass Supreme that has 71,000 miles. Since the battery has never acted up, is it really necessary?

—Marilyn

Tom: This is really a lifestyle question, Marilyn. Are you the kind of person whose day would be ruined if you got stranded somewhere, or would breaking down be a little adventure in an otherwise dull and dreary life?

Ray: If you got seven years out of your current battery, you've done very, very well. And you probably should expect it to die in the relatively near future. How soon? Who knows? It could be tomorrow, it could be a year from tomorrow. But it's certainly near the end of its useful life.

Tom: The question is, do you want to drive around with a brand-new battery, secure in the knowledge that your battery is not going to die and strand you? Or do you want to get every drop out of this battery and take your chances that some morning you'll come out and the battery will be dead? For some people, getting stuck like that is a terrible, awful experience, and they want to avoid it at all costs.

Ray: Then there are people like my brother's wife who look forward to it. She figures the next breakdown might be her chance to meet a handsome young tow-truck driver and finally dump my deadbeat brother!

THE RAT
WORE
PLAID

Horror Stories from the Showroom Floor

THE RAT WORE PLAID

Dear Tom and Ray:

I have a disturbing problem. I own a 1993 Buick Roadmaster. Recently, the "Service Engine Soon" light came on. I went back to the dealer who sold me the car. They couldn't take care of me right away, so the car had to stay there a few days. When they got to it, they found a dead rat in the heater duct. Of course, the rat was removed. But the service manager told me to be sure and keep my windows closed so the rat problem doesn't happen again. He said the rat had to get in the duct from the INSIDE of the car. Well, I never, ever open my windows except when I go to the bank. There was a bar of candy in my little litter box right in front of the heater opening, but it had not been chewed, so I see no evidence that a rat was inside the car. How do you suppose the rat got inside?

—*Maxie*

Tom: I think the rat got in at the dealership, Maxie. Did you ask them if they're missing any salesmen?

Ray: Whatever its origin, my guess is that it came in from the outside. Most rodents enter cars from the ventilation ducts, which are outside the car, right below the front windshield at the top of the engine compartment. The little varmints usually go in seeking warmth and protection from the elements. And unfortunately most of them don't get back out.

Tom: But if your dealer has determined that the rat was on the inside section of the ventilation system and that it had to have entered from the inside, then perhaps it got in while the car was at the dealership. They had the car for several days. Maybe they left the windows open?

Ray: There's only one way to find out for sure, Maxie. Ask for a description of the rat. If it was wearing plaid pants, white shoes, and a little white rat belt when they pulled it out, I would say it's definitely a dealership rat.

IS RUST ILLEGAL IN WISCONSIN?

Dear Tom and Ray:

I'm going to buy a new car—a black Toyota Camry—for use in Wisconsin. The dealer says the Toyota rust warranty is "essentially void" in Wisconsin because we use salt on the roads in the winter. Is he correct?

—**Rob**

Tom: No. He's full of baloney, Rob. Many states still use salt on their roads to improve traction. And while it's true that the salt does speed up the corrosion process, it does not void any manufacturer's warranty that we know of.

Ray: What he probably meant to say was that the warranty is "essentially useless." That's true. Most manufacturers offer a six-year or longer "rust-through" warranty. That doesn't mean they'll fix the car if it rusts. It only means they'll fix any part of the car that actually rusts *through*, i.e., where rust makes an actual hole right through the body.

Tom: So your car could have surface rust from bumper to bumper. You could have paint blistering all over the hood and a roof with the complexion of a two-day-old pizza, and the warranty wouldn't help you one bit—until the actual holes appeared.

Ray: So if you expect to take advantage of the rust-through warranty, Rob, at the first sign of rust, you might have to start *sprinkling* salt on those spots on a daily basis. And if you add a little sulfuric acid and a few well-placed nail holes, you might be able to get the thing to rust all the way through before the warranty runs out—but I wouldn't count on it.

YOURS ARE OLD, WORN, AND LOOSE, LADY

Dear Tom and Ray:

When I took my Honda Accord into the dealer last month for a new battery, they called me to say I needed new "front lower ball joints." Suspecting that they may just have had a boat payment due, I asked why they thought I needed these new ball joints. They said mine were old, worn, and loose. "Yeah," I said, "and what about the ball joints?" They said the ball joints were part of my suspension, so it was a possible safety issue. I frankly didn't go for it. So now I'm wondering, will my engine fall out onto the road while I'm driving? I hate that.

—Amy

Tom: Rest assured, Amy, bad ball joints will not make your engine fall out while you're driving. So you can completely erase that worry from your mind.

Ray: Bad ball joints can, however, make the wheels fall off. So if that concerns you at all, you might want to get them replaced.

Tom: This is actually a very common problem on Accords, so if I had to guess, I'd guess that the dealer is telling you the truth. And he's right—it is a safety issue—assuming you consider your front wheels "safety equipment."

Ray: Actually, I must say that I find it sad that we mechanics have such lousy reputations, that even when we tell someone like Amy the truth and try to warn her about impending doom, her response is "Yeah, sure, buddy!"

Tom: Well, after all those "dipstick polishing specials" we've sold over the years, you can't really blame Amy, can you?

Ray: I guess not. Get a second opinion if you want to, Amy, but I'd get the work done soon. And while you're at it, have the rear ball joints looked at too, promise?

I GOT YOUR UPSELL RIGHT HERE

Dear Tom and Ray:

I purchased a Honda Odyssey today and the dealer tried to sell me a $1,200 protective interior/exterior coating. I said no, but he said he would honor the offer till Monday. Should I buy this, or is it just an "upselling" strategy to get more money out of me?

—**Sally**

Ray: Tell him you're not interested, Sally. And then when he calls back and asks if you'd be interested if it was $600, tell him no again.

Tom: Exterior protection is unnecessary. The car already has exterior protection. It's called paint.

Ray: And the inside . . . well, that's a lost cause anyway. If you just bought a minivan, you probably have, what? Little kids! They spill milk, drop fruit, grind chocolate into carpets, and barf on the seats. And that's only the stuff you'll know about. Other than lining the whole interior with plastic or pulling the kids behind you in a U-Haul trailer, there's not much you can do to prevent that.

Tom: Well, you can get an interior that's the color of dirt. That helps.

Ray: Actually, you might try buying a few spray cans of Scotchgard and treating the seats and carpet occasionally. That might make it easier to clean up the inevitable messes, and that's essentially what the dealer is going to do for $1,200. You can do it for $12, and that's what we'd recommend, Sally.

OOPS!

Dear Tom and Ray:

On Sunday after church my wife and I got into our 1994 Thunderbird and started the car. It idled roughly and began missing and backfiring. On Monday morning I nursed the car to my local Ford dealer. He diagnosed the problem as a bad fuel injector at the No. 2 cylinder. Later I called to pick up the car and was told not to come in because the car had a miss that the mechanics wanted to investigate. The next day they would not return my calls. The following day they told me they had the engine out of my car and that the No. 2 connecting rod was bent. They told me they would replace the rod and the piston for $1,000. Apparently when they changed the fuel injector, the mechanic allowed the fuel to drain down into cylinder No. 2 and then hydro-locked it when he tried to start the car. What should I do?

—Raymond

Tom: I'd laugh at them, Raymond. I'd say, "That's funny, guys. You bent my connecting rod, you took my engine out without my permission, and you want me to pay for it? Good one, fellas!"

Ray: It certainly sounds like they're the ones who bent your connecting rod, Raymond. When you went in, you complained of missing and backfiring. A bad connecting rod would not have caused those symptoms. It would have caused an intense vibration. So unless it was vibrating badly when you went in, my guess is that after they changed the injector they accidentally bent the rod and then panicked.

Tom: That's when they weren't returning your calls. Every time the phone rang seven of them would run into the men's room and lock the door. We had to expand our men's room at the shop last year for this very reason.

Ray: But they don't have to hide from you. Repair shops carry insurance for bonehead mistakes like this. Why? Because mistakes happen. And these guys are going to have to make a claim on their bonehead policy and fix this for you for nothing.

Tom: If they don't offer to do that, tell them not to touch the car, and have it towed to an independent mechanic. Have him look at it for you, so you have a witness. Then I'd take the dealership to small-claims court. Based on your description, you'll almost certainly win.

Ray: But I don't think it's ever going to get that far. I think they were just trying it to see if you'd bite. Once you say no, I think they'll just say, "Oh, OK. We were just kidding." Especially after you drop the words "witness", "lawyer", and "small-claims court." Good luck, Raymond.

DOOR 1, 2, OR 3?

Dear Tom and Ray:

I would appreciate your opinion on a problem I had with my Ford F150. After shopping and returning to start my truck, I turned the ignition switch and the starter spun like an electric motor without turning the engine. AAA tried to start the truck with a jump start with the same result, so they hauled it to a Ford dealer. There the service advisor wrote up the work authorization, listing the problem as "no start, possible starter," with a preliminary estimate of $450. The next morning the service advisor called to say they didn't think I had a starter problem after all, but rather a dead battery and that they were going to try a quick charge. About half an hour later the advisor called to say my battery wouldn't take the charge, and that it appeared as though something had wiped out my battery, voltage regulator, alternator, and starter. It cost me $686. Does this sound plausible?

—Bob

Ray: Gee, Bob. It's highly unlikely that your battery, voltage regulator, alternator, and starter would all go bad at the same time by themselves. I mean, the chances of that are about the same as the chances someone would greet my brother as "Hey, handsome."

Tom: I would say there's a 99 percent probability that this was due to human error. The problem is, it's very hard to know who did it. But in the interests of vile innuendo, let us present three possible scenarios.

Ray: In the first scenario, "Moe," the AAA tow-truck driver, fries your electrical system. He recently graduated from the work-release program and his automotive skills are admittedly a bit rusty. And in the dark he accidentally hooks up the jumper cables backward. That sends a large jolt of electricity in the wrong direction, which puts the whole system in the meat locker.

Tom: In that scenario, "Larry," the dealership service advisor, listens to your description and assumes correctly that you're describing a starter problem. In the morning they discover that everything is fried, and you're out $686.

Ray: Scenario Two assumes Moe is innocent. In fact, he was the *Towboy* centerfold in October 1972. He knows that your starter gear isn't engaging and that you need a new starter. He knows a jump start won't help, but he does it anyway just to make you feel better (being the sweet guy that he is).

Tom: Then Moe tows your truck to the dealership where Larry, the service advisor, sizes you up, gives you an estimate of $450 for a $150 starter job, and watches your face. You don't flinch. He radios to the front office that he has a live one, and the next morning they call you and give you song and dance No. 38B and charge you $686.

Scenario Three maintains that both Moe and Larry are innocent. Larry gives you a ridiculously high quote on the starter purely by accident. He means to write "1," but instead he writes "4" for some subconscious reason understood only by Larry's mother and Sigmund Freud.

Ray: Next morning, "Curly," the mechanic, tries to start the truck and finds that, by coincidence, your battery is weak. Curly knows a weak battery won't cause the sound you described, but he doesn't trust you or Larry to give an accurate description of the problem, so he decides to start from scratch and jump-start the battery.

Tom: So he tells "Shemp," the nineteen-year-old "garage gopher," to hook up the jumper cables. Shemp has three jobs at the garage. He sweeps the floors, he gets coffee for the other mechanics, and he jump-starts cars. But sweeping floors is the only job he seems to have gotten the hang of.

Ray: So Shemp hooks up the jumper cables backward and fries the whole works. Then he plays Mickey the Dunce, and you end up paying $686.

Tom: You'll notice that all three of these scenarios have the same ending. And I'm afraid that's the ending you're going to have to settle for at this point. It's going to be awfully hard to prove what really happened, because the dealership and AAA can simply point the finger at each other.

Ray: You can try talking to them both, but without the help of Agent Jack Bauer I'd be very surprised if you get an admission of guilt from anybody. Sorry, Bob.

TWO TRUCKS ARE

CHEAPER

THAN ONE

And Other
Wacko Theories

TWO TRUCKS ARE CHEAPER THAN ONE

Dear Tom and Ray:

I read your column every week. Why, I don't know. I have to admit to a little envy. I'd love to get paid (you do get paid, don't you?) for writing smart-aleck answers to really dumb questions. Anyway, speaking of dumb questions, here's mine: Would it make any sense, or save any cents, to own two pickup trucks—one 2WD and one 4WD—and drive each of them for a six-month period each year? I currently own a 4WD Jeep pickup, which is great for winter driving. Driving it only during the winter would double its life expectancy, wouldn't it? And a 2WD pickup driven only in good weather should last even longer, right? Does this make any sense at all?

—Jim

Ray: Sure it does, Jim. Owning two things is always cheaper than owning one.

Tom: That's why most poor people own two homes. It's always cheaper to maintain two homes, one you use during the winter and one during the summer, because while a house is sitting idle, you're not putting all that wear and tear on it. Don't you think?

Ray: The same is true for big-screen TVs. One 52-inch TV is expensive, but if you buy two and watch each one only half the time, you'll really be piling up the savings.

Tom: Then there's wives. My accountant told me it's much cheaper to have two wives. So I got divorced, and all I pay for the first one is alimony! What a deal!

Ray: So by all means, if you want to save money, buy an extra pickup truck—and get another house or two while you're at it.

Tom: P.S., Jim. Do you believe we just got paid for giving you this smart-aleck answer?

SUFFERING FROM PBCSD

Dear Tom and Ray:

I have a brother-in-law who is neurotic. He thinks that if you drive on the highway for an hour, you have to let the car idle for half an hour with the hood up when you get to your destination. This is a man who also shakes his carbonated beverages before he opens them. Please tell my brother-in-law that neither of these practices are necessary.

—Nancy

Tom: Wow, Nancy. This guy needs professional help. He's obviously suffering from PBCSD: Post–British Car Stress Disorder. He must have spent his formative years driving something like an MG.

Ray: Yeah. He's obviously been traumatized by driving cars that were prone to overheating, and now he can't drive a real car across town without having flashbacks and leaving the hood up in the driveway for half an hour. He needs help!

Tom: We've had some success treating this disorder with cognitive behavior-modification therapy. It's similar to what they do for people who are afraid of flying.

Ray: You start by taking him out in a nice reliable Nissan and driving him around for fifteen minutes. Then you show him that the car hasn't overheated and caught fire yet. Next time, you drive him around for thirty minutes. And you slowly increase his time in the car until this fear of calamitous engine failure begins to subside.

Tom: You can do this, Nancy. Just take it a step at a time. And whatever you do, don't let him near an Alfa Romeo or a Renault. He may get retraumatized and have his recovery set back by years.

LET SLEEPING TRANSMISSIONS LIE

Dear Tom and Ray:

We recently contacted the local AAMCO transmission shop about servicing our 1992 Chevy Blazer's automatic transmission, which is working just fine. The vehicle has almost 100,000 miles of mostly highway driving. The AAMCO man said it should have been serviced every 25,000 miles and that it would now have scale deposits in the transmission, and that doing the service now would cause problems. He said if it were his car he would now do nothing to the transmission. We admit we've been negligent in letting it go this long, but is this guy right? It doesn't make sense to us.

—David and Patty

Tom: It doesn't make sense to us, either, guys. First of all, the recommended service interval for this transmission is 100,000 miles. So you're right on time. You haven't been negligent at all.

Ray: And I've never seen a recommendation from Chevy that calls for transmission service every 25,000 miles under normal conditions. That may be this particular AAMCO shop's recommendation because they'll make four times as much money if you do it that often. But I think the guy's wrong on that account.

Tom: This guy is also perpetuating the myth that "disturbing" an older transmission will somehow cause irreversible problems (this is also known as the "let sleeping transmissions lie" theory). This myth is based on the belief that the transmission has gotten used to its old, dirty fluid. And if you drain out that loving, old, comfortable, familiar fluid and introduce new, clean, uncaring, unfamiliar fluid, the transmission will be upset and won't remember how to work right. This, of course, is complete horse droppings. A transmission fluid and filter change is never harmful, no matter how many zillions of miles you have on the car or how many fish scales you have in there.

Ray: Scale deposits, not fish scales.

Tom: Whatever. David and Patty, you should go to another mechanic and tell him you are coming in for your 100,000-mile transmission service. And don't worry about a thing.

WILL HITTING MYSELF IN THE HEAD WITH A HAMMER GROW HAIR?

Dear Tom and Ray:

I do most of the light maintenance on my vehicle, and I've added a step in my oil changes that I think is beneficial in the long run. Here's what I do: I drain the warm, dirty oil, just like everybody else. Then I add this step: With the drain plug still out, I start the engine and let it idle for about a minute. I usually manage to get an extra cup or so of oil purged from the oil pump and related plumbing. My question is, am I doing more harm than good? I change the oil every 5,000 miles, and I figure the more dirty oil I can remove when changing the oil, the better.

—Ken

Tom: You want the good news first, Ken? You are significantly cutting down on the number of future oil changes you'll have to do on this car.

Ray: The bad news is that it's because you're going to croak the engine. This is a terrible idea, Ken.

Tom: You might have noticed that while you're running the engine to extract that last cup of oil, the oil light on your dashboard is on. You also might have noticed that there's a warning buzzer or chime that's sounding. Those are what we call "idiot lights," Ken. And they're speaking directly to you, buddy.

Ray: The light and buzzer come on when the oil pressure is so low that serious damage to the engine is probably occurring. When they come on, you're supposed to turn off the engine immediately to limit the damage.

Tom: Here's why: The key components of the engine are made of metal. And when the engine is on, they're spinning, or moving up and down hundreds of times a minute, even at idle. When they're moving they're rubbing against other pieces of metal. To prevent these things from destroying each other, there's an elaborate system that forces pressurized oil between all these moving parts whenever the engine is running. But that oil-pressure system can only work if there's (A) oil, and (B) pressure. You have neither.

Ray: Without oil, even for a minute, those parts scrape against each other and wear down. Then the damaged parts no longer fit together perfectly. Those gaps between parts make it harder to keep the oil pressure up, and it's a downhill spiral from there.

Tom: So it's absolutely not worth it, Ken. Leave that extra cup of dirty oil in there. It's irrelevant, especially when diluted with 4 quarts of brand-new oil.

Ray: And just cross your fingers that you haven't done too much damage yet. You can't, in good conscience, sell this car to anybody else. So you're just going to have to hang on to it and drive it into the ground. But don't worry, Ken. It won't be a long drive.

TOO MUCH TIME ON HANDS

Dear Tom and Ray:

I have a Chevy K10 Blazer with 140,000 miles on it. I would like to build or buy a spare tire mount for the front end of the vehicle. I have been thinking about purchasing one of those heavy steel grill guards designed to protect the front end from tree damage in off-road driving. Into the grill guard I would weld in cross-bracing to accommodate the spare tire. My concern centers around the needed air flow for the radiator. Will a spare tire mounted in the front block the air needed for the cooling system and cause damage?

—Tommy

Ray: Yes. And I'd advise against it. It will get in the way of the cooling system, and that will cause engine damage.

Tom: Plus, with a spare tire in the way, it's going to be hard to see where you're going. Although with that "tree guard," I guess that's not so important.

Ray: If you're considering a project like this, you obviously have too much time on your hands, Tommy. You need a hobby, and given the mileage on this Blazer, I'd suggest you take up engine rebuilding.

MARRIED TO A REAL PRINCE

Dear Tom and Ray:

My husband gets very upset with me if, when changing lanes, I pull the turn indicator lever into the full "on" position, necessitating manually turning it to the "off" position after the lane change. He says this severely damages the mechanism and if one is not making a sharp enough turn so the lever flips back to "off" as the car straightens out, one must only lightly tap the indicator so that it will return to "off" as soon as pressure is removed. I try to do it correctly, but sometimes if I don't concentrate or am in a hurry, I accidentally pull the lever fully on, and then I get a lot of sighs, shrugs, and sarcasm. None of the other women I know seem to have been told this. Can you tell me if this is true?

—Pat

Ray: Don't worry, Pat, you're not damaging the car. I mean, sure, every time you use the turn signal mechanism, you wear it out a teeny-tiny bit. But so what? Every time you get in and out of the car, you wear out the seats a little bit, too. But what are you going to do about that? Drive standing up?

Tom: This is really a dumb thing for your husband to worry about. First of all, I can't remember the last time we replaced a turn signal lever that had worn out. But more important, while you're worrying about the optimum finger pressure on the turn signal lever, you *should* be watching the road. How's your husband going to feel if his little turn signal lever works perfectly but the front end of his precious little car is smashed into the back of a UPS truck?

Ray: Tell him there are far more important things to worry about, like world peace and whether *The Office* is going to be back next season.

COUSIN BUBBA!

Dear Tom and Ray:

I recently got into a discussion with a friend about the volatility of fuels. He claimed that diesel fuel is highly volatile but gasoline is not. I told him it's the other way around. He said he knows that gasoline isn't volatile because his cousin Bubba puts out his cigarettes in a can of gasoline. I responded that what Bubba does sounds dangerous and highly unlikely. Now I'm afraid that my friend will try to duplicate Bubba's stunt. What should I advise him?

—Ken

Ray: Advise him to take out a nice, large life-insurance policy on Bubba, naming you and him as co-beneficiaries, Ken.

Tom: Here's why: The burning tip of a cigarette is somewhere between 750 and 1,100 degrees Fahrenheit, depending on whether you measure it on the side or in the middle where it's hottest. The ignition point of gasoline is only 500 to 860 degrees Fahrenheit. So, you do the math, Ken. Cigarette + Gasoline = Kaboom!

Ray: The truth is, it is possible to throw a lit cigarette into a bucket of liquid gasoline and have the cigarette go out. If the gasoline and/or ambient temperature is cool and the flame is extinguished quickly, you might luck out. But here's why you're taking an awfully big risk. . . .

Tom: Since gasoline is highly volatile—and you are correct, Ken, it's more volatile than diesel—it's continually giving off gasoline vapor. And gasoline vapor has a lower ignition point than liquid gasoline. So if your lit cigarette spends an extra half second in the gasoline vapor before getting into the liquid, or if it floats for a moment on top of the liquid before being extinguished, it could much more easily ignite the vapors, which would then ignite the whole thing. And that could lead to tragic—or in Bubba's case, Darwinian—consequences.

Ray: Diesel fuel is far less volatile, and it won't vaporize at room temperature. In fact, as far as volatility is concerned, diesel is the same thing as home heating oil—and it was chosen as a home heating fuel because of its relative safety. So you won't see diesel vapors igniting in the same way as gasoline vapors.

Tom: But still, I would strongly—make that very strongly—suggest to your friend that the surgeon general has determined that smoking, in and of itself, is a bad idea. And extinguishing your cigarettes in any kind of flammable liquid is a pretty clear demonstration of world-class stupidity.

Ray: And just to be on the safe side, Ken, since your friend might share some genetic material with his cousin Bubba, if you ever hear your friend utter the words "Hey guys, watch this!" run like hell.

STOP PUSHING MY BUTTONS

Dear Tom and Ray:

Both of our cars have trip odometers that we always forget to reset when starting out on a trip or when we just want to measure the distance from point A to point B. My husband insists that we pull to the side of the road before pushing the reset button. He says if it's pushed while the car is in motion, it will screw up the speedometer, the odometer, the cable, etc., etc., blah, blah, blah. I say the hell with it—just set it whenever you want. He's really pushing my buttons by insisting on this. What do you say?

—Jeanne

Ray: Jeanne, I don't mean anything bad by this, but your husband is a complete wacko.

Tom: Yeah. Usually, we try to defend (A) men, (B) husbands, and (C) people with wacko theories—all out of a sense of camaraderie. But we're at a loss with this guy, Jeanne.

Ray: You can hit the reset button on the odometer whenever you want. No damage at all will be done.

Tom: And by the way, if he tries to tell you that you have to pull over and shut off the car before changing radio stations, don't believe that one either.

ASSUME THE POSITION

Dear Tom and Ray:

It seems there are two schools of thought (mine and my husband's) on when the air-conditioner can be turned on with the engine running. I say it can be turned on at any speed. He says you need to slow down to at least 40 mph before flipping the switch. Am I right, or what?

—Jennie

Ray: You're right, Jennie. You're right, already!

Tom: This is a sore point for us, because we used to agree with your husband. We figured that since the air-conditioning compressor is run by a belt driven by the engine, you'd be better off turning it on at lower speeds, so you didn't "jolt" the compressor into action, right? After all, who likes to be jolted into action? Not me!

Ray: You? You don't even like to be gently lulled into action!

Tom: After we gave out this eminently plausible explanation on our NPR radio show a few months back, about a hundred air-conditioning technicians and engineers wrote to us and told us what morons we were.

Ray: And while we get that sort of feedback after every show, this time our critics had a viable counterargument. They said that since the air-conditioning compressor cycles on and off frequently on its own, it's designed to be "jolted" at any speed, at any time. According to lots of engineers who wrote to us, the compressor clutch is designed to be heavy-duty enough to take this punishment and is not at all bothered by being jolted to life at 60 mph.

Tom: So, Jennie, this means you have every right to ask your husband to "assume the position"—waistband up around his chest, shoulders shrugging demurely, chin down, eyes up, and muttering, "Yes, dear."

OUT OF THE CLOSET

Dear Tom and Ray:

I have been told that adding seven or eight naphthalene mothballs to a tank of gasoline increases the octane. Is this true? If it is true, what will it do to the engine of the vehicle?

—Donald

Ray: That's an excellent question, Donald. This mothball story has been around as long as we have. So immediately upon receiving your letter we called in the illustrious Jim Davis, Ph.D., director of the chemistry labs here at Car Talk Plaza, to try to get a definitive answer. And Jim said he'd get right on it.

Tom: Two months later he called us and apologized for the delay, which he said was unavoidable due to a two-month-long faculty meeting that had just ended at Harvard, where he moonlights.

Ray: Anyway, after several months of study and the complete depletion of an otherwise useful NSE grant, Jim has concluded that this mothball story is basically a bunch of horse pie.

Tom: There are several different types of mothballs on the market, none of which, to his knowledge, do anything to improve the performance of gasoline. They *will* burn, so you will get some power out of them. But since mothballs are more expensive than gasoline, this is not a very economical way to get to work, Donald.

Ray: If there were some magical performance-enhancing mothball, Jim says, don't you think Exxon and Mobil would be selling it to us as an expensive gasoline additive, i.e., "Mobil Super . . . Now with Mothballs!"

Tom: The kind of mothball you mention, Donald, is made of naphthalene, which is a hydrocarbon, like gasoline. For those chemical engineers reading today, it's $C_{10}H_8$, and it looks like two benzene rings fused together. Jim says that benzene makes a very smoky fire when burned, so his guess is that naphthalene would make a lousy gasoline. On the other hand, he says, since it's just carbon and hydrogen (like gasoline), naphthalene probably wouldn't do any harm to the engine, either.

Ray: Another type of mothball that could potentially hurt things is made of dichlorobenzene. That won't improve your car's performance either, but since it throws chlorine into the mix, it can produce HCl as a byproduct when burned.

Tom: For those of you who don't remember your high school chemistry, HCl is hydrochloric acid, the stuff that burns through almost anything it touches. And pumping HCl through your engine and exhaust system is probably not very good for its longevity, Donald.

Ray: Not to mention what it does to (A) the people who happen to be breathing anywhere near the end of that exhaust system, (B) your catalytic converter, and (C) your manufacturer's warranty.

Tom: So, based upon Jim's research, we feel confident in summarily dismissing the notion that adding mothballs to your gas tank does anything to improve performance.

Ray: The only thing Jim will guarantee is that if you put mothballs in your gas tank, any sweaters you store in there will come out without moth holes in them.

CHEAPSKATE ALERT

Dear Tom and Ray:

My father is always telling me to turn my windshield wipers down or off whenever possible. He says they will wear into the windshield glass, especially at high speed. Is this true?

—Jessica

Tom: Your father is an unmitigated cheapskate, isn't he, Jessica? I'll bet he lets the dog lick the dinner plates just to save money on dish soap.

Ray: Technically, he's right, of course. And I would do exactly what he says, Jessica. He wants you to turn off the windshield wipers whenever possible. Fine. Whenever it's sunny out, you turn 'em off. That's when it's possible.

Tom: The wipers do grind a little bit of dirt into the windshield, shortening its life by some amount. But you need the wipers when it's raining so you can see. And that should always be your primary consideration. If the wipers help you see better, use them. If they don't, turn them off. And if the windshield ever gets so scratchy that you have trouble seeing out of it at night or in the rain, get a new windshield. Most experts agree that seeing is a crucial part of driving.

Ray: And if Dad ever starts talking to you about using the brakes less often so you won't wear out the pads, write to us again and we'll have a little talk with the old guy, okay, Jessica?

REMORSEFUL SALESMAN

Dear Tom and Ray:

We've just purchased a new Ford Ranger pickup. The salesman told us the air-conditioner should be turned off before turning off the ignition when we park. He said something about it making the O-rings last longer. We could find nothing in the owner's manual about this. What do you think?

—Joyce

Ray: Well, this salesman is obviously a rocket scientist. He must have worked on NASA's space shuttle program, since he's so intimately familiar with O-ring technology.

Tom: Actually, he's nuts, Joyce. I think he's suffering from PMS: Post-Manipulation Syndrome. He knows he's just done a song and dance and talked you into buying all kinds of stuff you don't need: the power moonroof, the pin-striping, the crushed Corinthian interior. And now that he's actually talked you out of your money, he's feeling a little bit remorseful.

Ray: Not remorseful enough to give you any of it back. But he does want to ease his conscience by giving you something. So what does he give you? Advice.

Tom: Lame advice, as it turns out, but advice nonetheless. Turning off the air-conditioner before you turn off the engine makes no difference to the air-conditioner or the engine.

Ray: He probably doesn't even know his advice is useless. He's in a remorseful, cathartic trance after the sale, so he really can't be held responsible for his actions. Just pat him on the shoulder and tell him to give a hundred bucks to charity when he comes to.

THE DEAR DEPARTED WAS WACKO

Dear Tom and Ray:

My dear, departed daddy told me that if you broke in a new car engine at slow speeds, it would always be slow and sluggish. Is this true? What's the real skinny? Is there a preferred break-in protocol?

—Susan

Tom: Great question, Susan. But since we never speak ill of the departed, we can't answer it.

Ray: Actually, I'm sure your daddy was right about many other things and was a superior human being in all other regards.

Tom: But his story about break-in is an old myth, Susan. And we don't know how it got started. Probably by some teenage boy who got caught racing his dad's new car.

Ray: It assumes that the car somehow "learns" to go slow when it's young and then it never knows how to go at normal speeds later on. Kind of like my brother at work.

Tom: But it's just not true. There is a legitimate protocol for breaking in a new vehicle. It varies slightly from car to car, but the main purpose is to allow the piston rings to "seat," or conform to the exact shape of the cylinder walls so that they make a tight seal. And most experts agree that the best way to do this is to keep the engine rpm below 3,000 and to vary the engine speed (i.e., don't drive at one constant speed for a long time).

Ray: And the break-in period generally lasts anywhere from five hundred to one thousand miles. Or until your check clears at the dealership, whichever comes first.

Tom: If the piston rings don't seat correctly, your car might burn oil later on. And nobody wants that.

Ray: So the speed at which you break the car in might have an effect on how much oil it burns. But it has absolutely no effect on how fast or slow the car goes.

Tom: Last time we checked, that was mostly affected by the position of your foot on the gas pedal.

WHAT'S THE PLURAL OF "LEXUS"?

The Really Big Questions

WHAT'S THE PLURAL OF "LEXUS"?

Dear Tom and Ray:

My husband and I recently had a question we thought you might be able to answer. This question is a little offbeat, but we're curious. What is the plural of "Lexus"?

—Amy

Tom: Well, Amy, the problem is, nobody knows, because no one's ever been able to afford more than one Lexus. So we'll just have to speculate.

Ray: We suspect that the root of *Lexus* is Latin. And we traced it back to one of two possible roots. One is Latin for "half-price Mercedes." And the other, roughly translated, means "Japanese Buick." My guess is it's probably the former.

Tom: Also, sticking with Latin, we see two possible declensions. There's the "opus" model, of which the plural is "opera." So if we follow that rule, the plural of *Lexus* would be *Lexera*. One Lexus, two Lexera.

Ray: More likely, *Lexus* follows the same rule as *Taurus*, which pluralizes as *Tauri*. So we'd have one Lexus, and two Lexi. Personally, I think that sounds classier.

Tom: And as soon as we find a Latin scholar who owns more than one Lexus, Amy, we'll give you the definitive answer.

COMPLETELY METRIC

Dear Tom and Ray:

I am confused about the meaning of the term "liters." What does it mean? Is a high liter rating better than a low one? My car says 2.0 liters.

—**Frank**

Tom: A liter is a metric measure of volume, Frank. It's a little larger than a quart. If you go to your supermarket and head over to the soda aisle, you'll see that those real big bottles of Coke are 2.0 liters. The same size as your engine!

Ray: Actually, the engine itself isn't that size, 2.0 liters is a measure of the engine's displacement—that is, the total amount of space in all the empty cylinders. So if you took out all four spark plugs and one by one set each piston at the bottom and filled the cylinders with Coke, you'd have just enough Coke in that two-liter bottle to fill them all up. And, who knows, you might make the car run better, too.

Tom: What the displacement tells you, Frank, is approximately how much power the engine can produce.

Ray: It's not an exact measure, because some 1.8-liter engines actually produce more power that some 2.0-liter engines, because of other mechanical differences. But generally speaking, a 3.0-liter engine is going to be more powerful than a 2.0-liter engine because it can burn more gasoline for each revolution of the engine.

Tom: And which is better? That really depends on the car. A big, heavy Lincoln Town Car with a 2.0-liter engine would be a complete dog. But a Saturn with its 1.9-liter engine has plenty of power. It's kind of like a hat, Frank. You don't necessarily want the biggest one; you want the one that fits.

Ray: Except in my brother's case. Then you want the one that covers as much of his face as possible.

BITS, BYTES, AND BONDING

Dear Tom and Ray:

Can you tell me why the auto industry puts computers in cars? What is the advantage? It used to be that any mechanically minded person with experience could repair a car. Now, of course, it is necessary to take the car to the dealer or to a factory-authorized repair shop that has factory-trained mechanics. Was this the reason computers were introduced?

—Margaret

Tom: Yes. Back in 1983, a secret meeting was held in Paducah, Kentucky, between mechanics, bankers, and the chairmen of the Big Three. It turns out that mechanics across the country were falling behind in their boat payments, and bankers brought the three parties together because they didn't know what they would do with all those thousands of repossessed boats. By the end of that meeting they resolved to make cars so complicated that no one would be able to work on one in a driveway again. Then the mechanics would get more business, the bankers would get their boat payments, and everyone would be happy. I think Oliver Stone is working on the screenplay as we speak.

Ray: My brother's being a wise guy, Margaret. No one specifically set out to make cars more complicated. But they certainly have gotten that way. The main reasons for computers are emissions controls and improved fuel economy.

Tom: Computers allow cars to have sophisticated fuel-injection and engine-management systems that would never have been possible with carburetors. Through the use of various sensors, the computer can tell how dense the air is, how cold the engine is, how hard you're stepping on the accelerator, and whether you flossed your teeth before you left for work—and can calculate from all this data the precise amount of fuel to send into the cylinders. That means minimal waste of fuel and a lot less pollution. Not to mention better performance and greater reliability.

Ray: But it has come at a cost. In my opinion, a social cost more than an economic one. Tinkering with cars used to be a great American pastime. Guys would spend Saturdays out in the driveway taking things apart, and then trying to put them back together before it got dark. And that's no longer possible.

Tom: And I don't think we realize the widespread ramifications of this change. For example, what do those guys who used to work on their cars do now? They sit around watching TV, feeling useless, and picking fights with their wives. So the increase in the divorce rate is directly attributable to the introduction of computers in cars.

Ray: Tinkering with cars also used to present an opportunity for father-child bonding. That's gone, too. And when parents aren't directly involved in their kids' lives, we all know the crime and drug abuse rates go way up.

Tom: Laundry detergents used to be sold on their ability to remove grease. Where did that grease come from? From engines on Saturday afternoon! And the clothes that couldn't be "Fabbed" and "Duzzed" and "Whisked" fueled the entire Goodwill industry. Gone now, due to computers in cars.

Ray: Plus, being out in the driveway gave neighbors an opportunity to meet and get to know each other. This would often lead to socializing, the building of communities, and invitations to barbecues.

Tom: That's right. So the decrease in the sales of red meat can also be laid at the feet of computers in cars.

Ray: There's the hope for the future! As soon as the American Beef Association figures this out, they're going see a major lobbying effort to bring back the carburetor—probably with a series of TV ads starring Clint Eastwood. I think your worries are over, Margaret.

CAR WON'T START? RENT A BAY!

Dear Tom and Ray:

A friend of mine was in Germany, where they have garage bays you can rent out to do some work on your car yourself. This seems like a great idea. Can you provide me with information on why these do not exist in America? What are the unforeseen obstacles to starting up such a business?

—Heather

Ray: Well, the first obstacle is that you can't make any money at it. At least we couldn't.

Tom: We came up with this same exact idea back around 1973. We opened a place called "Hackers Haven," where people could rent our bays and our tools, and fix their own cars.

Ray: We figured it was a "can't miss" idea. We saw ourselves standing around in white lab coats and collecting the money while people lay under their own cars and banged their own heads on transmission housings.

Tom: But, alas, it didn't work out that way. You see, most people needed help. They would call us over and ask us questions. And before we knew it, we were helping them fix their cars. And then they were standing around in white lab coats and we were banging our heads on their transmissions.

Ray: So after a couple years of that, we decided that if we were going to fix the cars anyway, we might as well charge money for it. And we turned the place into a regular old repair shop.

Tom: And, to tell you the truth, I think it would be even harder nowadays to make such a concept work. First of all, cars have gotten a lot more complicated in the past thirty years. A guy used to be able to come in and do his own brake job if he knew a thing or two. But nobody's going to come in today and fix his own ABS.

Ray: Moreover, with people getting sued for serving hot coffee these days, the insurance costs would absolutely croak you. Can you imagine? You call up Frank, your insurance agent, and ask how much your coverage would be. He asks you, "What kind of dangers are your customers going to be exposed to?"

Tom: And you say, "Oh, nothing serious, Frank . . . cars falling off lifts onto their heads, batteries exploding in their faces, hot oil pouring down their arms . . . oh, and occasional asphyxiation from carbon monoxide. Hello? Frank?"

WHEN LESS TRACTION IS MORE

Dear Tom and Ray:

I own a '99 Pontiac Grand Prix with traction control, which makes sense to have in the Midwest, my fair region. There is a button on the dash that allows me to turn it off, should I desire to do so. I travel and rent cars frequently, and I've noticed that other makes that have traction control have an on/off button as well. Why, in the name of Britney Spears' burgeoning midriff, is this the case? Under what circumstances would the average driver turn it off, and would he or she know when the proper circumstances arise? I certainly don't!

—Larry

Tom: Good question, Larry. High-school kids were finding it impossible to "do doughnuts" in the school parking lot with their dad's traction-control-equipped cars, so the automakers thoughtfully added an on/off switch.

Ray: Actually, the off switch is for situations where the traction control works too well. Traction control prevents the wheels from spinning when you accelerate. This prevents the driven wheels from breaking away and skidding.

Tom: But there are a few rare circumstances in which you might want the wheels to spin. One is if you're stuck in the snow. If you're stuck in the snow with the traction control on, here's what happens: The wheels will try to turn, they'll get no traction and they'll stop. So in a situation like that, the traction control can prevent the wheels from turning at all. No traction, no power to the wheels!

Ray: So by turning off the traction control, you can allow the wheels to spin and you can try to get out of the snow the old-fashioned way—by rocking the car back and forth . . . and digging a two-foot hole under each wheel that you'll never get out of.

Tom: It's possible that by turning off the traction control, you can create a little momentum and blow out of a pile of snow. The same thing can happen in sand or mud, too.

Ray: But other than that, just leave the traction control on and let it do its job.

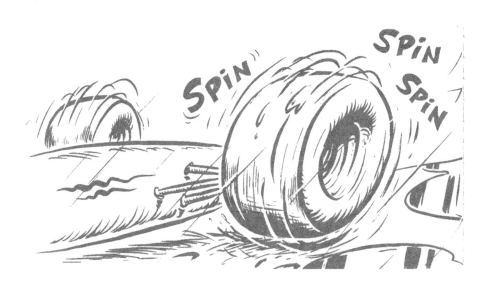

EGGS PRESTONE

Dear Tom and Ray:

I love your column, guys. I'm curious about a rerun of MacGyver that I saw last week. He was trying to escape from "San Arugula" or someplace south of the border. He found an abandoned jeep and of course got it to fire right up. However, the radiator was riddled with bullet holes, so he thought he was a goner. Then his little lightbulb went off. He stole some chicken eggs from a nearby farm, and with the engine running, he proceeded to separate the eggs, putting only the egg whites in the radiator. Voila! The leaks were sealed, he escaped, and he once again saved the world. My obvious question: Would that really work? I know you're laughing, but you have no idea how many things I've "MacGyvered" with paper clips, so who knows? Just wondering if I should keep a few eggs in the toolbox.

—Ruth

Tom: Great question, Ruth. In the old days, we would have dumped the whole egg in there, yolk and all. But now that we're all worried about cholesterol and heart disease, most repair shops have switched over to just egg whites.

Ray: Actually, it might work. Here's the theory: If there's a small hole in the radiator, the water or coolant is going to escape through that hole. When you dump in the egg, it goes in as a gooey liquid. But as it travels through the hot fluid (note: engine running), it cooks and hardens. And if everything works just right, the egg is dragged toward the hole, hits it, hardens up, and plugs the leak.

Tom: That's the theory. People have also used pepper flakes for this repair, which I also keep—along with the eggs—in my toolbox. Even if I don't have a radiator leak, it's nice to know I can always whip myself up a half-decent breakfast.

Ray: The egg trick can actually work, Ruth, as a temporary fix, if the hole— or holes—are small enough.

Tom: But I'm afraid it won't work on bullet holes. The radiator is not a single tank that holds water. The part of the radiator that holds the coolant comprises a bunch of thin metal tubes. Those tubes carry the coolant slowly from one end of the radiator to the other. It's during that journey that the heat is removed.

Ray: But those little tubes are only about an eighth of an inch wide and an inch deep. And if a bullet blows through one of those tubes, it's going to literally tear it in half, leaving a 38-caliber gap between the two remaining pieces. And even a Western omelet won't fix that.

Tom: I suppose that if a bullet just grazed a tube, it might still work. So, let's assume, for the sake of MacGyver's reputation, that the hail of bullets just nicked one of the cooling tubes. Otherwise, that would have been MacGyver's last episode, Ruth.

WHAT'S IN A NAME?

Dear Tom and Ray:

We were wondering why so many carmakers use names that end with "a"? For example, Supra, Corsica, Honda, Daytona, Maxima, Beretta, Miata, etc. Do the carmakers just have an incredible lack of imagination?

—Anthony and Dan

Tom: We discussed this with our staff grammarian, I.M. Shirley Wright, who told us that there are good reasons for this practice. While there are exceptions, most cars whose names ended in consonants have been miserable failures. AMC is a case in point. They made the Rambler, the Pacer, the Hornet, the Matador, the Ambassador—and look what happened to them! (Incidentally, the vice president for car names at AMC must have come over to Chrysler when Chrysler bought AMC, because Chrysler then started producing the Shadow, the Spirit, and the Horizon.)

Ray: Once carmakers discovered this, they made a quick decision to switch to vowels. The question was which vowel? *E* was too French, and French cars have never sold well in the United States. The French association was great when it came to selling wine, fries, and poodles, but it didn't sell cars. Chevette, for example, is not one of the outstanding name plates in automotive history.

Tom: The letter *i* was discarded because it suggested pluralism. At one point, Pontiac considered calling the Fiero the Fieri, but market research revealed that people weren't sure whether they were supposed to buy one Fiero or two Fieri.

Ray: The Americans never considered *u* very seriously either, because it sounded too Japanese. So the Impalu and the Electru were ruled out almost immediately. However, it's a little known fact that all the Japanese cars were originally supposed to end in *u*. Luckily, their American marketing executives talked them out of it. But we almost had the Hondu, Corollu, Mazdu, and the Korean-built Ford Festivu.

Tom: That left only *o* and *a*. *O* is masculine, and it worked for a few macho cars like the Camaro and the Yugo, but cars are traditionally thought of as female—like ships—so ending with *a* was the obvious choice. Voila!

OUR MANIFOLD COOKING IDEAS

Dear Tom and Ray:

When are you guys going to come out with a cookbook? It's a natural.

—*John*

Ray: We're working on it, John. We've got a number of recipes in development.

Tom: For instance, my brother is perfecting his Rack and Pinion of Lamb recipe. He's also working on his Chile con Car.

Ray: I also have a lovely Linguini with Fram Sauce, Chicken with Rosemary and Timing, Pork Shocks, and Steamed Mussel Cars.

Tom: We have Pasta Carbureta, Blackened Red Starter (cajun style), Veal Scalopinging, and, for those special occasions, Lobster Thermostat.

Ray: You want a side dish? How about Scalloped Tires? Or try our Horn on the Cob, Manifold Roasted Potatoes, or a helping of Pasta with Prestone Sauce.

Tom: We have dessert, too. How about some Strawberry Short Block? An Apple Won't Turnover is nice. Or try our Vroom Raisin Pudding.

Ray: Breakfast, you say? Oil-pan Cakes? Or some Steering Links?

Tom: If you've got other ideas for our cookbook, send them to us via our Web site, Cartalk.com. Who knows, we may even get around to publishing it someday.

QUESTIONABLE

CAR-MA

Issues of Automotive Etiquette

QUESTIONABLE CAR-MA

Dear Tom and Ray:

Help! I think I'm in deep doo-doo. The two-year lease on my Jeep Cherokee is about to expire. I did the unthinkable: I unhooked the odometer cable at the transmission. But after 3,000 miles, my conscience won out and I reconnected it. I'm still over my mileage allowance by about 3,000 miles. I realize it was a big mistake, and I want to make restitution, but don't know how to approach it. My question is, how much trouble am I in? Would buying the vehicle eliminate the problem? When I return the vehicle, will they be able to tell the mileage has been tampered with? Thanks.

—Gary

Ray: Geez, Gary. It's not often that we get e-mail from criminals! This is very exciting! I hope it's okay that I forwarded your little note right on to www.fbi.gov/life-prison/no-parole.

Tom: You committed fraud, Gary. And even though you attempted to cheat a car dealer, we still don't approve of your actions.

Ray: Chances are the dealer won't know that you disconnected the odometer cable. Some cables do have a painted seal on them so you can tell when they've been disconnected. But in this case the dealer probably doesn't have reason to suspect you. If you came in after two years with 29 miles on the thing, he might get suspicious. But I'd say it's unlikely he'll investigate a car that's 3,000 miles over the limit. But you never know.

Tom: Unfortunately, even if it does get past him, he's just going to turn around and sell the car to some other poor unsuspecting customer who doesn't know the car has extra miles on it. And that will certainly bring you bad automotive karma for many years to come.

Ray: So the only way out of it is for you to buy the car, Gary. And then you'll have two choices. Once the statute of limitations is up, you can sell the car and disclose the actual mileage then. Most states require you to notify a buyer if you have reason to believe that the odometer does not reflect the actual mileage of the vehicle. That way you're not actively committing fraud. And in that case, having to explain the discrepancy and admit that you've been a sleazeball in a past life will be your penance.

Tom: Or, you can just keep the car until the bitter end. Then, having driven around in a Jeep Cherokee for 150,000 miles, you will have paid your debt to society, your chiropractor, and the Chrysler Corporation—and then some.

FLASH THIS, PAL

Dear Tom and Ray:

My boyfriend and I are having an argument about people who roar up behind you and flash their lights frantically until you pull over so they can zoom by. I think this is rude and he thinks it's perfectly acceptable. I will certainly pull over to the right if there's space to do so. However, most of the time when this happens, traffic is heavy and I'm already going 5 to 10 mph over the speed limit and the joker behind me keeps flashing his lights as if doing this will enable me to pull over more quickly. This drives me crazy! When did this become an acceptable way to behave on the highway? Please tell me if I need to get with the program and accept this as stan-dard "polite behavior" or if I can tell my boyfriend to never do this again. Thanks.

—Kathie

Tom: I wouldn't bother telling him anything, Kathie. I would simply dump his sorry butt. This guy's a jerk.

Ray: And my brother knows a lot about jerks, Kathie. He's self-actualized.

Tom: This is absolutely not polite, acceptable behavior. It's very obnoxious, rude, testosterone-poisoned, self-centered, and dangerous behavior. It's also illegal behavior, because when he comes up on another car's bumper and flashes his lights, he's tailgating. He probably doesn't even know that tailgating's illegal.

Ray: It's one thing if a person is driving at or below the speed limit in the pass-ing lane and you'd like to pass. Then, if there's room for him to pull over, it's our opinion that it's acceptable behavior to pull up (without tailgating) and give the guy a moment to notice you in his rearview mirror. If he doesn't pull over, then you're allowed to flash the lights once and wait a reasonable amount of time for him to comfortably and safely get out of the way. But just trying to intimidate other drivers via obnoxious tailgating and light flashing is unacceptable, pure and simple.

Tom: And Kathie, you know it's only a matter of time before this guy's boorish behavior shows up in other parts of your life. Can you imagine having a baby with this guy? You'll be in the delivery room and he'll bang on the door and say, "C'mon, Kathie! Push harder! I've got a football game to watch this afternoon!"

HOW TO COMMIT ROAD RAGE, LESSON NO. 1

Dear Tom and Ray:

Today I was involved in an accident. I was happily cruising along at the speed limit (35 mph) in the right lane when someone came up behind me. He was clearly very upset that I was doing just the speed limit, and he could not stand being unable to get around me because of a line of cars in the other lane. He began to follow me very closely. Now this situation activated some kind of psychological trigger for me, and I responded by tapping my brakes, causing him to swerve into the other lane (fortunately, there was a gap in the line of cars there). He didn't stay there, though. He swerved back into my lane, and followed me even more closely. I responded by applying my brakes gently, and he proceeded to hit my car—four times before we came to a stop! I got out of the car and started yelling at him, which he reacted to by leaving the scene—fortunately, I was able to get his license number. There was no visible damage to my car, but I filed a police report anyway. Now, legally, I know the accident is entirely his fault. But ethically, I feel I could have avoided the accident if I had not reacted in such a rash way. I have come to the conclusion that I react this way because I feel like I am being bullied, and I do not like being pushed around. I am normally a totally nonaggressive driver who gives everyone lots of room and who drives at the speed limit, even when I feel that I would like to be going a lot faster. My question is, can you suggest an alternate, less self-destructive but equally satisfying response other than hitting the brakes when I am being tailgated?

—Cliff

Ray: You want something equally as satisfying as having him crash into your car four times and then take off? Well, you could drive into a tree to make him feel bad.

Tom: Unfortunately, the only reasonable thing to do in that situation is ignore the guy, Cliff.

Ray: That's difficult to do when somebody is being an unmitigated jerk and riding up on your butt like that. But if you're doing the speed limit and driving legally, that's the only good solution.

Tom: Anything else is escalation—and, as you realized, that makes you equally responsible for the results. He does one thing; you retaliate by doing something else. Then he retaliates, and pretty soon you two are the Hamas and Hezbollah of Route 95—and nobody even remembers, or cares, who started it.

Ray: It's very tempting to "teach the other guy a lesson." But that's not your job. My brother tried that for years. When someone would tailgate him, he'd stop the car in the middle of the road, get out, walk around, and ask if there was a problem. After being punched in the nose five or six times and paying off the vacation homes of several local plastic surgeons, he finally gave up and now leaves the lessons to the police.

Tom: That's what you need to do, too, Cliff. You need to put your faith in karma. Or car-ma, in this case. When something like this happens, remember that people ultimately get what they deserve, even if it isn't at that exact moment. If you're a nice person, good things will happen to you. If you're a jerk, the police will eventually pull you over, you'll get a $200 ticket, your insurance rates will go up $400 a year, a guy at the gym will put itching powder in your shorts, and you'll end up with a rash on your butt in the shape of New Jersey. That's the way the world works, Cliff.

Ray: And if you don't believe me, ask my brother to bend over, drop trou, and show you how to get to Trenton.

HOW TO SEND A MESSAGE

Dear Tom and Ray:

The other night just after dusk I was driving and noticed a dark-colored car driving behind me in the same direction without its headlights on. It was actually difficult to see the car except when it passed directly under a streetlight. I wanted to signal the driver to turn on his lights but was not sure how to do it. So I slowed down enough that he passed me. Then when he was in front of me I flashed my headlights several times from low beams to high beams. He still didn't turn on his headlights. Soon thereafter we both had to stop at a traffic light. So I pulled up next to him, opened my window, and called out to him that he needed to turn on his headlights. He hollered back to me, road-rage style, something to the effect that he was angry at me for "high-beaming" him. I would have thought he would thank me for reminding him about his headlights. He was a jerk, but I didn't want to see him cause an accident just because his car could not be seen in traffic. So what should I have done, and what should I do in a similar situation next time?

—Carol

Tom: This is a situation we've all been in, Carol. The first thing you need to realize is that anyone driving at night without his lights on probably has other things on his mind. He's not 100 percent focused on the task at hand.

Ray: What I usually do—rather than flash my high beams—is turn my lights off and then back on again several times. But in my experience, it usually takes five or six different cars to get through to someone whose lights are off. So understand, Carol, it's not your sole responsibility to get the message across. It takes a village, in this case.

Tom: You turn your lights off and on, and then another good citizen turns his lights off and on, and so on. And then the guy with his lights off finally says to himself, "Hey, why is everybody turning their lights off and . . . d'oh!" That's how the message finally gets through.

Ray: I'd adjust your technique, Carol. But your heart was in the right place. It's just that the lightless guy ahead of you was thinking about the spool of plastic line from his weed whacker that got caught up in the cuff of his trousers and de-pantsed him on the front lawn while a school bus full of teenagers was driving by with their cell-phone cameras, and now he's the most-forwarded video on the Internet. You did what you could, Carol. Rest easy.

BULLETS OVER BURBANK

Dear Tom and Ray:

I live in Los Angeles. I have a '93 Honda Civic Del Sol with 127,000 miles. Last week when I was driving home from work at 75 mph on the southbound 405 freeway, someone in a passing car on my left or someone in an oncoming car fired a shotgun. The bullet, a .40-caliber, went through the door and hit me in the chest, then ricocheted and fell onto my seat. I suffered no injuries. The Special Investigative Unit is now handling the incident. My question is, what is the cost of fixing the bullet hole in the door of this car? How easy is it to do, and is it worth it? What kind of financial impact does it pose to the value of my car if I want to sell it or trade it in?

—Ellen

Ray: Good thing you decided to get those Kevlar implants, Ellen!

Tom: Fix it?? Are you nuts, Ellen? A bullet pierces the car, hits you on the chest, and bounces off! You walk away, completely unharmed! That car gave its own sheet metal to save your life. How could you even think of fixing it?

Ray: Plus, on a more practical level, you'll be a guy magnet with this story, Ellen. Imagine what happens when some guy asks about the bullet hole. You tell him about being shot at, and how the car saved your life. You'll be a celebrity down at the local tavern in no time.

Tom: Most of all, it's a reminder of what could have happened. Every time you get in your car, you'll be forced to remember that you almost didn't make it home that day. It's a reminder that every day is precious and you have to live life to the fullest. So I wouldn't even dream of fixing it, Ellen.

Ray: And since the value of the car is a concern, I'd guess the car is worth about $4,000 if you fix the hole, Ellen, and $4,100 if you don't.

CAR TALK STAFF

Airline Seat Tester	Wilma Butfit
Alignment Inspector	Lou Segusi
Assistant Customer Care Representative	Kurt Reply
Audience Counter	Hugh Wake
Audience Estimator	Adam Illion
Audience Response Analyst	Luke Warm
Automotive Medical Researcher	Dr. Denton Fender
Automotive Registrar	Megan Model
Auto Seat Tester	Fitz Matush
Blues Coordinator	Mahamadan Ptolemy
Brother in the Military	Major Payne-Diaz
Car Talk *Bouncer*	Euripedes Ibreakayourface
Chairman, Underemployment Study Group	Art Majors
Chicken Soup Provisioner	Kent Hoyt
Chief Accountant	Candace B. Rittenoff
Chief Counsel	Hugh Louis Dewey of Dewey, Cheetham & Howe
Clothing Designer	Hugh Jass
Co-Chairmen of Apathy Study Group	Ben Thayer, Don Thatt
Coordinator of Summer Visits to the In-laws	Don Juan-Gogh
Copyright Attorney	Pat Pending
Corporate Spokesperson	Hugh Lyon Sack

Crash Tester	Hope Anna Prayer
Credit Counselor	Max Stout
Curator of Tom's Car Collection	Rex Galore
Customer Car Care Representative	Haywood Jabuzoff
Designer of Casual Clothing Line	Noh Tie, Woo
Director of Gender Studies	Amanda B. Reckondwyth
Director of Listener Support	Noah Fundrive
Director of Speed Bumps	Slow-Me-Down Milosevic
Divorce Attorney	Carmine Nottyors
Document Security Expert from Jamaica	Euripedes Upmann
Dope Slap Administrator	Thad Hertz
Emissions Tester	Justin Hale VII (I, II,III, IV, V, VI may they RIP)
Food Taster	Howard M. Burgers
Grammar Consultant	I.M. Shirley Wright
Guest Accommodations	The Horseshoe Road Inn
Head of Our Working Mother Support Group	Erasmus B. Dragon
Liaison to the British Isles	Isaiah Oldchap
Liaison to the Space Program	Roger Houston

Little Dog of Payne-Diaz family	Toto Payne-Diaz
Montana Traffic Law Director	Hugh Jim Bissell
Mortgage Loan Consultant	Nora Lenderbee
Optometric Firm	C. F. Eye Care
Personal Hygiene Advisor from the Tokyo Office	Oh Takashawa
Personal Makeup Artist	Bud Tuggli
Proprietor of Car Talk's Men Clothing Store	Euripedes Eumenedes
Public Opinion Pollster	Paul Murky of Murky Research
Ralph Kramden Impersonator	Mohammed Ahamana Hamana
Ratings Analysis Specialist	Rita Menweip
Russian Chauffeur	Picov Andropov
Seat Cushion Tester	Mike Easter
Second Shift Meteorologist	Claudio Vernight
Shop Foreman	Luke Bizzy
Staff Butler, from the Car Talk Bombay Division	Mahatma Coat
Staff Disciplinarian	Tara Neuwon

Teenage Daughter	Sasha Royal Payne-Diaz
Two-Year-Old	Ariel Payne-Diaz
Videographer, Tel Aviv Office	Schlomo Replay
Wardrobe Consultant	Natalie Attired
Windshield Wiper Replacement Team	Ike and Zeke Leerley

INDEX

A

Acura, 20, 115
Africa, traveling in, 136, 140–41
Air-conditioners, 80, 167, 171
AMC, 14, 16, 186
Antitheft devices, 56–57
Aston Martin, 20–21

B

Backfiring, 70, 150
Ball joints, 148
Batteries
 on concrete floors, 68–69
 cutoff device for, 62–63
 jump-starting, 32, 71, 152, 153
 radio use and, 32
 replacing, 142
Block heaters, 105
Bounciness, 108
Boyfriends, rude, 194–95
Brakes, 46–47, 53
Brothers, younger, 34, 100
Buick, 146
Bullets-ripping-through-your-car-like-paper problem, 140, 200
Butts
 expanding, 93
 hot, 90–91

C

Carburetors, 98
Cars
 breaking in new, 172–73
 dirty, 94–95
 maintenance costs of, 26
 names of, 186–87
 as personality tests, 122–23
 for pizza delivery, 12–13
 purchasing, 12–13, 20–21, 28–29, 132–33, 136
 re-teaching, 82–83
 ruining, 24, 42
 stolen, 56–57
 Tom and Ray's, 14–15
 washing, 30–31
 worst, 16
Car Talk staff, 202–5
Cheapskates, 46–47, 123, 170
"Check Engine" light, 44–45
Chevy, 16, 60, 70, 82, 118–19, 137, 138–39, 158, 162
Clutches
 downshifting and, 52

 nonworking, 137
 riding, 24
Cold starts, 42–43, 104–5
College students, 26, 28–29
Commissioned Salesperson Syndrome, 107
Compounding, 117
Computers, 178–79
Connecting rods, bad, 150
Cookbook ideas, 188

D

Dads
 cheap, 170
 manipulating, 24–25
 parenting tips for, 36–37
 punchy, 33
 questionable advice from, 98, 170, 172–73
Dead bodies, 86
Dealers, questionable practices of, 148–53, 171
Diesel engines, 18–19, 64
Diesel fuel, 164–65
Differential, 118–19
Dodge, 16, 17, 24–25, 27, 70, 128, 138–39
Do-it-yourself repair facilities, 180–81
Downshifting, 52–53

E

Emblems, 38
Emissions tester, 81
Engines
 breaking in, 172–73
 cold starts for, 42–43, 104–5
 diesel, 18–19, 64
 moving, 89
 rebuilding, 60–61
 ruined, 48, 51, 60, 160–61
 size of, 177
 warming up, 104–5
Equipment decals, 119
Exhaust system. See also Mufflers; Tail pipes
 short drives and, 27
 smoke from, 60–61, 70
 thudding noise from, 86–87
 water in, 30–31

F

Fans, 115
Felipo Berrio test, 119
Fiat, 17
Ford, 16, 50, 54, 76, 90, 106, 138–39, 150, 171

Frantz Filter, 65
Friends, loser, 71, 164–65
Fuel economy, 12, 72–73, 178–79

G
Garage, sleeping in, 88, 89
Gasoline. *See also* Fuel economy
    additives, 70
    mothballs in, 168–69
    putting out cigarettes in, 164–65
    smell, 80–81
    volatility of, 164–65
Girlfriends
    car problems of, 112–13
    disagreements with, 126–27
    dumping, 115
    neglected, 116–17

H
Handling, 108
Head gaskets, 60
Headlights
    driving without, 198–99
    flashing, 194–95, 198
    left on, 62–63
    water in, 106–7
Hills
    braking and, 53
    starting and, 112–13
Honda, 15, 51, 71, 122, 134–35, 148, 149, 200
Husbands
    advice from, 104, 163
    crazy, 70, 124–25, 163, 166
    disagreements between wives and, 128, 167
Hyundai, 13

I
Idiot lights, 160
Idling
    after driving, 157
    rough, 150
Ignition switch
    accessory position, 32
    faulty, 88–89
Indicator lights, 82–83, 163
Interior protection, 149

J
Jeep, 28, 182
Jerks, 36–37, 94–95, 102–3, 194–98
Jump-starting, 32, 71, 152, 153

K
Kids. *See also* Teenagers
    destructive, 30–31, 38, 149

    sadistic, 33
Kill switches, 56–57

L
Ladies, little old, 80
Land Rover, 136
Leather seats, 54–55
"Let sleeping transmissions lie" theory, 158–59
Lexus, 93, 176
Limited slip differential, 118–19
"Liters," meaning of, 177
Locking differential, 119
Locks, picking, 34–35
Lock-up torque converter, 103

M
MacGyver repair tips, 184–85
Male Answer Syndrome, 106–7
Mazda, 30, 56
Mechanics
    arguing with, 68–69
    getting a date with, 120–21
    incompetent, 48–49, 76, 150–53
    reputation of, 148
    talking to, 102–3
Meetings on Tuesday. *See* "Monday Meeting"
Men. *See also* Boyfriends, rude; Brothers, younger; Dads;
    Husbands
    automotive knowledge of, 99, 102–3
    bonding rituals among, 98
    communication among, 100–101
    judging, from their cars, 122–23
    Male Answer Syndrome, 106–7
Mercury, 32, 88
MG, 15, 122, 132–33, 157
Midlife crises, 124–25, 134–35
"Monday Meeting," 6–8
Mothballs, 78, 168–69
Motor mounts, 89
Mufflers, 30, 92

N
NHTSA (National Highway Traffic Safety Administration), 90
Nissan, 51, 116–17
Noises
    backfiring, 70, 150
    rattling, 128
    thudding, 86–87
NTSB (National Transportation Safety Board), 90

O
Odometers, 166, 182–83
Oil
    burning, 60–61, 70
    changing, 64–65, 160–61

driving without, 48–49, 160–61
filters, 50, 64–65
in gas tank, 70
plastic ring in, 84–85
Oldsmobile, 102–3, 108, 142
Overdrive, 126–27
Overheating, 157
Owner's manual, finding, 44

P

Paint
oxidation of, 116–17
scratches in, 94–95
PBCSD (Post–British Car Stress Disorder), 157
Pickup trucks, 18–19, 116–19, 156
Pizza-delivery vehicles, 12–13
PMS (Post-Manipulation Syndrome), 171
Police, trouble with, 36, 38
Pontiac, 80, 182
Positraction, 118–19
Power curve, 124–25
Punch Buggy, 33

R

Radiator hoses, 78–79
Radiator leaks, 184–85
Radios, 32, 88–89
Rats, 78–79, 146
Rattles, 128
Recalls, 90
Relationship advice, 105, 115, 116, 126–27, 194–95
Reverse, driving in, 88–89, 137, 140–41
Road rage, 196–97, 198, 200
"Rockford," doing a, 141
Rustproofing, 66–67

S

Safety complaints, 90
Saturn, 44, 84–85, 124
Scratches, 94–95
Seats
leather, 54–55
replacing, 93
warmers for, 90–91
"Service Engine Soon" light, 44–45
Shifting, 52–53, 124–27
Shocks, 108
Short drives, 27, 43
Smoke, 60–61, 70
Spare tire mounts, 162
Spark plugs, tightening, 76–77
Spoilers, 114
Sports cars, old, 132–33
Stalling, 102–3
Starter bushings, 112–13

Starting
cold, 42–43, 104–5
difficulties with, 112–13, 150
Stolen cars, 56–57
Stunt driving, 141
Subaru, 78, 122–23
Suspension, 108, 148
Swaying, 108

T

Tailgating, 194–95, 196–97
Tailpipes
hairy, 92
water in, 30–31
Teenagers
choosing vehicle for, 28–29
driving vs. walking, 27
embarrassed, 24–25
good-driving incentive for, 36–37
radios and, 32
Tickets, 36
Timing belts, 51
Tires, 108
Toilet-paper filters, 64–65
Toyota, 12, 46, 52, 62, 126, 134, 136, 140, 147
Traction control, 182–83
Transmission, 103, 126–27, 158–59
Trip odometers, 166
Triumph, 132–33
Turn signals, 82–83, 163

V

Vans, 134–35, 138–39
Ventilation system, rodents in, 146
Volkswagen, 12, 16, 26, 33, 38, 112–13, 134–35, 138–39

W

Warranties, rust-through, 147
Water
in exhaust system, 30–31
in headlights, 107
Westheimer, Dr. Ruth, 116
Wheels, falling off, 148
Windshield wipers, 170
Winter driving, 42–43, 104–5, 182–83
Wives
always right, 99, 167
cheap, 46
disagreements between husbands and, 128, 167
hot-butted, 90–91
safety device for, 88
testing by, 20–21
Women. *See also* Girlfriends; Ladies, little old; Wives
attracting attention of, 52, 53, 108, 114
superiority of, 99